Industry and Higher Education

Industry and Higher Education

Collaboration to improve students'
learning and training

Edited by
Peter W. G. Wright

The Society for Research into Higher Education
& Open University Press

Open University Press
Celtic Court
22 Ballmoor
Buckingham
MK18 1XW

and
1900 Frost Road, Suite 101
Bristol, PA 19007, USA

First Published 1990

British Library Cataloguing in Publication Data

Industry and higher education: collaboration to improve
    students' learning and training.
    1. Great Britain. Higher education. Relations with industries
    I. Wright, Peter W. G.   II. Society for Research into higher education
    378.103

    ISBN 0-335-09635-2

Library of Congress Cataloging-in-Publication Data

Industry and higher education: collaboration to improve students' learning and
    training/edited by Peter Wright.
        p. cm.
      ISBN 0-335-09635-2 (hardback)
      1. Industry and education.   I. Wright, Peter.
    LC1085.I485   1990
    378.1′ 03—dc20   90-40017 CIP

Papers published in advance of the Society for Research into Higher
Education's Annual Conference on Industry and Higher Education held at and
in association with the University of Surrey, December 1990.

Typeset by Rowland Phototypesetting Limited,
Bury St Edmunds, Suffolk
Printed in Great Britain by St Edmundsbury Press Limited,
Bury St Edmunds, Suffolk

Contents

Part 4: Changes in Culture and Organization

List of Contributors

Ann Bailey is Higher Education Office Manager for the Digital Equipment Company in the UK. She started her career as a trainee in pharmacy, worked in general management, personnel and training, and studied part-time at Manchester Polytechnic and the Salford College of Technology to become a member of the Institute of Personnel Management. In her current post, she is responsible for establishing links with higher educational institutions throughout the UK. Her aim is to promote the development of the personal transferable skills that employers will need during the 1990s. She believes that this will involve changes in the way that academic knowledge is taught that can only be achieved by close collaboration between higher education and employers.

Robert F. Bud is Curator of Biotechnology and Head of Collection Services at the Science Museum. He obtained his PhD from the University of Pennsylvania in the history of science, and has a special interest in the relationship between science and industry. He has been responsible for organizing the Science Museum's galleries on the Chemical Industry, Plastics and Petroleum. His publications include: *Chemistry in America 1876–1976: Historical Indicators*, with A. Thackray, P. Thomas Carroll and J. Sturchio (Reidel, 1985), and *Science Versus Practice: Chemistry in Victorian England*, with Gerrylynn K. Roberts, (Manchester University Press, 1984). Currently he is engaged in writing a history of biotechnology.

John Fielden is the partner in charge of the Educational Practice of KPMG Peat Marwick Management Consultants. He has been active in educational consultancy in many countries, particularly in universities, for more than 20 years. After reading modern history at Oxford University he qualified as a chartered accountant and then took a 2-year research fellowship to study the management of universities in the UK and USA. Recently, he has directed a series of six handbooks on collaboration between business and higher education published by the Department of Trade and Industry and the Council for Industry and Higher Education.

Anne Jones is Director of Educational Programmes at the Training Agency (formerly the Manpower Services Commission, MSC). Previously, she has worked as a teacher, school counsellor, and Chair of one of the MSC's Area Manpower Boards. She was Head of Vauxhall Manor School, London (1974–81) and of Cranford Community School (1981–7). She has written and broadcast extensively. Her publications include: *Counselling Adolescents: School and After* (2nd edn, Kogan Page, 1984) and *Leadership for Tomorrow's Schools* (Blackwell, 1987). Her responsibilities at the Training Agency cover the Technical and Vocational Education Initiative (TVEI), Work-related Further Education, Compacts, and Higher Education (including the Enterprise in Higher Education Initiative).

Cari Loder is Research Officer in the Centre for Higher Education Studies (CHES) at the Institute of Education, University of London. She has worked at the Commonwealth Secretariat and the Overseas Students' Trust, acted as Consultant for the European Cultural Foundation, and participated in consultancies for the World Bank, OECD, ESRC, DES and PCFC. Her most recent publications include: *An Examination of Student Placements in Industrial and Commercial Enterprises* (1987), a report for the European Institute of Education and Social Policy; *Teaching Quality in Higher Education* (1989), a review of research and literature for the PCFC Committee on Teaching Quality; *Finding Facts Fast* (Penguin, in press). She is the editor of *Quality Control and Public Accountability in Higher Education* (Kogan Page, forthcoming).

Roy Lowe is Senior Lecturer in Education at the University of Birmingham, before which he taught in schools and colleges. He edits *History of Education* and is author of several books and numerous articles on English education over the last century, including *Education in the Post-War Years* (Routledge, 1989). He organized the 1986 Annual Conference of the History of Education Society on the theme of 'Higher education since industrialisation', and published its proceedings in *History of Education*, **16**(3), 1987. He is currently working on a social history of English education since 1964.

Peter Meyer-Dohm is Director of the Central Training Organization of Volks-wagen AG, Wolfsburg, and Honorary Professor of the Ruhr University, Bochum. He studied economics and social sciences at the Universities of Göttingen and Hamburg from 1950 to 1954 and was awarded a Diploma of Economics and Doctorate of Political Sciences. He was a Research Associate to Professor Karl Schiller, University of Hamburg from 1955 to 1964, in which year he qualified as *Privatdozent* there. He was Professor of Political Economy, the Ruhr University, Bochum from 1965 to 1981.

Gerrylynn K. Roberts is Lecturer in the Department of History of Science and Technology at the Open University, where her course work includes *The Rise of Scientific Europe, 1500–1800*. She graduated in chemistry at Vassar College and was awarded her PhD in the history of science at Johns Hopkins University. Her research focuses on the social relations of science and technology in Britain, especially with regard to chemistry, and she has a particular interest in the development of scientific and technological education. Her publications include: *Science versus Practice: Chemistry in Victorian England*, with Robert Bud (Manchester University Press, 1984), and contributions to C. Chant (ed.), *Science, Technology and Everyday Life, 1870–1950* (Routledge, 1989).

Peter Slee is Director of Enterprise in Higher Education at the University of Durham. He trained as a historian at the Universities of Reading and Cambridge and began practising at the University of Manchester before moving, via Durham University, to become Head of Education Policy at the Confederation of British Industries. As Director of Durham's EHE project, he is active in clarifying the contribution that HE makes to the development of highly capable members of the future workforce. His publications include: *Learning and a Liberal Education* (Manchester University Press, 1986); A consensus framework for higher education, in C. J. E. Ball and H. Eggins (eds), *Higher Education in the 1990s* (SRHE/Open University Press, 1989); and Concern for skills, *Universities Quarterly*, **40**(2), 1986.

Keith Tribe is Senior Lecturer in Economic History at the University of Keele. He graduated at the University of Essex and received a PhD at the University of Cambridge and was visiting Humboldt Fellow at the Institut für Soziologie, Heidelberg and Visiting Fellow at the Max Planck Institut für Geschichte, Göttingen. His most recent major publications are *Governing Economy: The Reformation of German Economic Discourse 1750–1840* (Cambridge University Press, 1988) and, as editor, *Reading Weber* (Routledge, 1989). His current principal research interest is the development of economic and commercial education in the UK 1870–1940, from which he has developed a more general interest in higher educational policy.

Gareth Williams is Professor of Educational Administration and Head of the Centre for Higher Education Studies at the Institute of Education, University of London. He is the author of several books and numerous articles on academic and financial aspects of higher education during the last 25 years. He was Director of the SRHE-Leverhulme programme of Studies on the Future of Higher Education in the early 1980s. His concern with business and higher education is an aspect of a long-run interest in understanding and assisting in the development of ways in which higher educational institutions can respond to the changing needs of society while maintaining their essential long-term values.

Peter W. G. Wright is Higher Education Adviser at the Training Agency, on secondment from Portsmouth Polytechnic. He graduated in sociology at the London School of Economics, received a master's degree in political sociology and a PhD in the sociology of knowledge. He has taught in an art college, three polytechnics and a university and spent a year in the Maison des Sciences de l'Homme, Paris. He is editor, with A. Treacher, of *The Problem of Medical Knowledge: Examining the Social Construction of Medicine* (Edinburgh University Press, 1982), and has published numerous articles including: Access or exclusion: Some comments on the history and future prospects of continuing education in England, *Studies in Higher Education* (1989), **14**(1), 23–40; Putting learning at the centre of higher education, in O. Fulton (ed.), *Access and Institutional Change* (SRHE/Open University Press, 1989). He is co-editor of *Higher Education Quarterly*. His research interest lies in the professionalization of knowledge in higher education.

1

Introduction: Crossing the Border, or Creating a Shared Territory?

Peter W. G. Wright

Over the last few years, the view that industry and higher education should work more closely together has come to be an all-but-unshakeable part of the dominant, conventional wisdom. Like other ideas that have acquired that status, the exhortation to industry and higher education to collaborate, has sometimes become scarcely more than an unthinking platitude with little bearing on action. And yet it should not: there are, indeed, cogent reasons why the world of work and the academic world should join forces; and there is much to be said about the circumstances in which such cooperation is likely to prove appropriate and fruitful, and those where it will not.

If we are to understand why close collaboration has not always taken place in the past or why, when it did, it has – on occasion – been unsuccessful, we shall need to understand the particular factors that have shaped British higher education and employment in their present forms. We shall need, too, to analyse their interests and values to determine both what may bind them together and what should cause them to remain distinct.

The aim of this volume of essays – specially commissioned in preparation for the 1990 Annual Conference, on 'Industry and Higher Education', of the Society for Research into Higher Education – is to make a contribution to the understanding of such issues. It sets out to consider the contexts in which higher education and industry (understood in the very widest sense of all employment in the private, public and voluntary sectors) now find themselves, and to examine various possible spheres of joint activity.

In doing so, it concentrates primarily on the contribution that both partners could make to improving the quality of students' learning and to increasing its relevance to the needs of employment. As a result, almost no consideration is given to research, consultancy or the transfer of technology, despite their great importance. This is for two reasons: first, these topics are already reasonably well recognized and investigated; secondly, to avoid overlap with the subject matter of the 1991 Annual Conference of the Society for Research into Higher Education, which will be specifically devoted to research.

In order to place the contributions in this volume in context, it may be useful to begin by considering some of the factors that have given rise to the pressure for employers and higher education to come together.

In one sense, of course, they have never been apart: it is possible to make a convincing case that higher education and employment have always been closely linked. Did not the medieval universities, it could be argued, arise directly out of the need to train clerics? Is it not easy to demonstrate the importance of the practice of medicine to Padua or Edinburgh, of agricultural concerns to the American Land Grant institutions, or of local industrial needs to the foundation of the British 'Red Brick' universities? Indeed, it is. None the less, despite these examples, the late nineteenth and early twentieth centuries were also the time in which the academic profession established itself and began to assert a dominant – and to some extent exclusive – influence over the higher education system: ... what A. H. Halsey has termed the model of the 'University of the Professors' (Halsey, 1986). Thus, the move towards greater closeness to industry can be seen as a real shift towards some new model.

Although this shift may have been more marked in some countries than in others, it is common, I would contend, to all developed societies and is driven by five broadly identifiable forces.

The first, and most obvious, derives from the rapid advance of technological knowledge and the related growth of the sophistication and complexity of the productive process. This, inevitably, gives rise to demand for a more highly skilled workforce and for a constant flow into industry of research and development.

The second, perhaps less obvious, is the movement from elite to mass higher education. In the past, when the academy directed its activities at only a tiny segment of the age group – often those who were regarded as the future elite of academics, senior civil servants, literary figures and other intellectuals – it could afford to give little attention to the needs of employment, especially when the latter made comparatively little use of knowledge-intensive technology. Today, in contrast, the overwhelming majority of graduates go into an enormous range of, generally, non-elite occupations; and, increasingly, the higher educational system is beginning to draw its clientele from those already in employment.

Thirdly, with the rise of new mass media, together with the decline of traditional elites and their associated systems of values (as well as the prevalence of deferential attitudes towards them), there has been a general – somewhat populist – tendency to challenge the ascendancy of professions (and their claims to be guardians of the public interest), not least that of the academic profession. The academy has increasingly found itself under pressure to address the needs of its consumers (itself a novel notion) and to consider the process of higher education as an enterprise shared with many others – now, significantly, often referred to as stakeholders (governments, community groups, students, parents and, of course, employers).

Fourthly, there are some signs that the changing social and cultural environment is beginning to form new conceptions of education, quality and personal fulfilment. Just as Humboldt's or Newman's visions of the university were born of the experience of the nineteenth century – especially out of responses to the growth of scientific knowledge and industrialization – so one might expect a different vision of higher education to emerge in the late twentieth-century world under the sway of powerful international currents and the dizzying growth of information technology and communications. The increasing currency of concepts such as competence, capability or enterprise might be interpreted as signs of an attempt to reformulate a conception of education that would be in tune with the special circumstances of the age that is now coming into being.

Finally, there is the force of internationalism. The growing integration of the world economy – not least through improved means of communication, the resultant sharpening of international competition, and the moves towards trans-national political union in Europe – means that no country can easily stand aloof from the tendencies manifested in the most economically successful. The fact that the USA and Japan are both countries which, in their different ways, give great emphasis to education, and where the links between industry and academia are substantial, necessarily increases the pressure on all other countries to follow suit.

This volume begins with Roy Lowe's account of the relationship between industry and higher education over, roughly, the last century. In it, he argues that – at least until recently – there has been a powerful tendency for all higher educational innovation in England to be curbed and redirected away from the needs of employment towards a particularly elitist conception of liberal education. Although he is able to recognize the advent of new forces for change, his conclusion is generally equivocal, if not pessimistic: 'The evidence of the most recent hundred years', he concludes, 'does not give grounds for unbridled optimism'.

Robert Bud and Gerrylynn Roberts, however, place another construction on data from much the same period. They agree with Lowe that nineteenth-century science came to be dominated by what they call a 'science college', or liberal educational model, rather than a 'polytechnic', or industrially relevant model. This, they interpret not as the resultant of deep social forces, but rather as the unintended consequence of a – perhaps, in retrospect, misguided – attempt to establish a '. . . practical scientific education [that] could be publicly provided in a way acceptable and useful to private industry'.

In their investigation of one particular kind of link between employment and academia – the industrial funding of higher education – Gareth Williams and Cari Loder try to estimate the extent of such funding in Britain, and to explore some of the dilemmas that it conjures up. They conclude by leaving the reader to decide whether the mounting stress on industrial funding has unleashed forces that are ultimately incompatible with the core features of liberal higher education as it has developed over the last 500 years or so.

Keith Tribe then analyses one of the paradigms commonly proffered as a model for British higher education in the next century, that of the USA. In his view, the accounts of that system often grossly distorted its reality. Although, for example, the US system is not uncommonly presented as an exemplar of private funding, in fact his figures suggest that, even in private institutions, direct individual and corporate funding only accounts for 14.6% of revenue – a figure not greatly dissimilar from non-state support in Britain and other European countries.

The next article, by Peter Meyer-Dohm, is the attempt of an industrialist with intimate personal knowledge and lengthy experience of the academic world to ponder its role and essential characteristics. He suggests that, to prosper, higher education must be responsive to the needs of industry yet remain detached from them. He sums this up epigrammatically: 'Detachment without receptiveness turns into isolation, receptiveness without detachment into a failure to carry out the scientific task.'

In the next contribution, Ann Bailey makes a fervent plea for higher education to give more attention to the fostering of personal transferable skills in its students, and to do so in close partnership with employers. This, she contends, will be essential if students are to acquire the qualities needed by those high-technology industries that are likely to become increasingly dominant in the years ahead.

John Fielden then draws on his rich experience of consultancy with higher educational institutions to examine the changes taking place in their culture and their relationship to what is happening in industry as a whole. He stimulates the reader to consider a question not far removed from that raised by Peter Meyer-Dohm: namely, do the changes now taking place in the management of higher educational institutions really represent a thorough understanding of the complex pattern of similarities and dissimilarities between the mission of higher education and that of other kinds of organizations?

Next, Anne Jones surveys the wide range of changes that are currently taking place in British education and links these to one major programme aimed at bringing about strategic curriculum development in British higher education: the Training Agency's Enterprise in Higher Education Initiative. In her opinion, the British higher educational world is on the brink of fundamental changes that will propel it into a closer relationship with employers and into cultivating imaginative forms of student-centred learning, relevant to its local settings.

The final contributor, Peter Slee, essays futurology. He explores various assumptions about the nature of British higher education by considering their implications for a series of predictions concerning its future. In the long term, he believes that a higher education based on the traditional ERIC (Education, Research, Instruction and Culture) will come to triumph over one based on the parvenu ERNI (Enterprise, Retrenchment, National Goals and Instrumentalism). Whether that is a pessimistic or an optimistic conclusion is for readers to decide.

In conclusion, it may be worth trying to draw out one assumption which, I believe, is common to all the contributors to this volume. This concerns the nature of the relationship which is desirable between the world of higher education and that of industry (or rather, more accurately, employment). A common thread in all the articles in this collection is the belief that higher education and industry really do share some significant common goals, which are as much a product of their distinctive differences as of their similarity; and that the experience of work is, in itself, one particularly valuable theatre of learning.

From this follow certain conclusions about how best to conceptualize the relationship of the two spheres. I want to suggest that most discussions of the links between higher education and industry are cast in terms of one, or more, of three distinct analogies. They are those of conquest, tourism and joint nationality.

The conquest analogy simply assumes that if one part could force the other to accept all its values, and assimilate its practices entirely to its own, all would be well. Although once, perhaps, this might have been framed as an injunction to industry to copy higher education, today its most familiar manifestation is the assertion – sometimes even fondly regarded in the academy – that higher education should be exactly like industry. Its deficiency is, of course, blindingly obvious: if higher education could find its salvation by aping industry, why are its services in demand at present? Its special virtues must, to some degree, lie in its being distinct from industry, not exactly like it.

The second analogy, that of tourism, is also familiar. It results in exhortations to both employers and academics to have more contact with the other. Contact, it is assumed, is a good thing in itself. But this is to be doubted: why should contrived contact between industrialists and higher educationalists lead to mutual understanding and collaboration any more than package holidays on the Costa del Sol should cause the British to have a deep empathetic penetration of Spanish culture. Unfocused and purposeless contact is every bit as likely to reinforce stereotypes as to dispel them.

What is needed, I would contend, is a practice based on what I would describe as the analogy of joint nationality. That is to say, a state of affairs in which employers and academics come together to share, and to carry through to conclusion, tasks that had not previously belonged to either party, and which would only be capable of achievement through the collaboration of both. These might involve projects to use the work place as a learning environment, attempts to assess and reward learning acquired in work, or the joint definition of measures of capability. Their common feature is that they would not simply involve academics or employers moving across a boundary into the territory of the other, but would involve the collaborative creation of a new sphere of activity. This, in my judgement, is where successful cooperation between the two partners is most likely to occur.

Reference

Halsey, A. H. (1986). Chairman's summing up. *Higher Education Newsletter*, **11**, 68–76.

Part 1

How the Relationship between Industry
and Higher Education has Taken Shape

2

Educating for Industry: The Historical Role of Higher Education in England

Roy Lowe

The first industrial revolution made comparatively few demands of the formal education system. During the late eighteenth and early nineteenth centuries, the development of the transport, textile, mining and iron industries in Britain called for new expertise which was often developed 'on the job', and created a need for a labour force which was disciplined and orderly but which required only minimal standards of literacy and numeracy. Many of the pioneers who devised new processes and techniques had themselves received only the barest of educations, or else had been educated at Scottish universities or in Dissenting Academies, since there was a complete absence of the teaching of 'really useful knowledge' in the English universities. Provincial scientific societies, such as the Lunar Society in Birmingham, rather than the ancient universities, were the intellectual forcing grounds of this transformation. The fact that industrialists looked to the developing system of schools to provide workers who were sober, industrious and compliant was an important factor which helped determine the scope and orientation of popular education during its first major growth phase. The outcome was a system, deeply influenced by the churches, which felt little need to bother itself with technological skills. This has proved to be an enduring and pervasive legacy, colouring subsequent developments and attitudes in higher education as well as at schools level.

It is hardly surprising, then, that this first industrialization elicited little response from the universities, which were in any case small and few. A succession of university dons defended the isolation of the universities from these developments, perceiving the ideal of a liberal education as paramount. As Mill emphasized in his famous inaugural as Rector of St. Andrews, 'the industrial arts . . . are not part of what every generation owes to the next, as that on which its civilization and worth will principally depend' (Sanderson, 1972, p. 5). This was echoed by Mark Pattison in 1876, when he told the Social Science Congress that:

it is no part of the proper business of a university to be a professional school. Universities are not to fit men for some proper mode of gaining a livelihood; their object is not to teach law or divinity, banking or engineering, but to cultivate the mind and form the intelligence (Sanderson, 1972, p. 5).

Although this period saw university foundations in Durham and London, the power of this orthodoxy, together with the small scale of these institutions, virtually guaranteed that they stayed aloof from industrialization, and were only marginal to the development of the professions. With only 50 or so students at Durham in its early years and less than 3000 at Oxbridge, it is understandable that, as late as 1870, the clientele of these institutions was predominantly 'the nobility, the landed gentry and the urban patriciate' (Jarausch, 1983, p. 24; see also Wright, 1989), and their curricula focused on classics and pure mathematics.

The second industrial revolution, which extended roughly from 1870 to the end of the First World War, involved the development of far more complex industrial processes. The ability to produce high-quality steel in quantity enabled the swift growth of the machine tool industry, and infant chemical, electrical and motor car production industries began to appear in Britain.

The fact that, in each case, these were matched by emergent competitor industries abroad placed an added premium on the acquisition of the necessary skills if these concerns were to be staffed and to develop. These developments in industry were matched by, and generated a significant growth in the professions: the new concerns needed their own administrative staff as well as the services of banks, insurance firms and the like. A further precondition of a reorientation of higher education was that the redistribution of population during the nineteenth century had created vast industrial townships in the north of the country that were completely isolated from the universities. Briefly, the local Mechanics' Institutes, Athenaeums and Literary and Philosophical Societies that sprang up in these towns seemed to hold out the hope of an indigenous system of higher education which might meet these industrial and commercial needs. But these were soon colonized by local professional elites who used them for social purposes, or else modelled their educational provision on that of the ancient universities.

By the 1870s, a situation had developed which many saw as little less than critical. Now a few enlightened industrialists began either to lobby for the development of technical education through bodies such as the National Association for the Promotion of Social Science or else by founding new institutions of higher education themselves. 'Who frequent our universities?' asked John Percival of the NAPSS in 1870. Then, answering his own question, he responded:

Not the men who are directing the life of Manchester, Newcastle, Liverpool, Bristol or Birmingham, but the sons of country gentlemen or men destined for certain professions, or a few sons of the wealthier merchants and manufacturers; whilst the names of Oxford and Cambridge are strange names to the mass of those who are guiding our industrial and commercial enterprise. . . . Who can fail to lament the want of real living connections between our old universities and the great commercial and industrial centres? (Lowe, 1987).

New civic universities were set up in an attempt to remedy this crisis. The first, Owens College, Manchester, was endowed by a businessman who was as much influenced by the Oxbridge ideal as by the needs of industry in the region. However, during the late 1860s, money flooded in from local industrialists: a Professorship in Engineering was endowed in 1866. Henry Roscoe, appointed as Professor of Chemistry, was a key figure in winning the support of cotton manufacturers, as Manchester's growing university college drew closer to local industrial and commercial needs. Elsewhere, the relationships were less ambiguous. In Liverpool, shipowners, industrial chemists and food manufacturers were the moving force. The Yorkshire College of Science at Leeds had Obadiah Nussey, a textile manufacturer and James Kitson, the locomotive engineer as its founding fathers. Firth College in Sheffield took its name from the steel magnate who endowed it and, from its inception, established scientific chairs linking with local industry. Similarly at Birmingham, Josiah Mason, pen manufacturer and pioneer of electroplating, founded a college with a strong orientation towards applied science. Mason went so far as to exclude the teaching of Arts subjects from his college. There was a similar involvement of industrialists in Newcastle, Bristol and Nottingham too (see Sanderson, 1972, ch. 3).

At first glance, the appearance of these new colleges, and their promotion to full university status during the first few years of the twentieth century, may seem to mark a resolution of this longstanding crisis. But, in reality, the problems surrounding the relationship of higher education with industry and the professions were, if anything, exacerbated at the turn of the century, through the fact that what was emerging was, for the first time, identifiably a system of higher education with characteristics that were to shape its relationship with industry and the professions for much of the twentieth century.

At the apex of this developing system stood the Universities of Oxford and Cambridge, which now began to forge a new and lasting relationship with the major professions. Although the Law Society (founded in 1825) and the Inns of Court retained control over entry to the legal profession, the establishment of a School of Jurisprudence at Oxford in 1850 and the appointment of a succession of eminent jurists to chairs at both universities ensured that, by the final years of the nineteenth century, it was most unusual for men to enter an Inn of Court without first attending one or other of the ancient universities. The reform of entry to the upper echelons of the civil service, in the wake of the Trevelyan-Northcote Report of 1854, resulted in admission to the 'first division' of civil service grades being through a competitive examination modelled closely on the honours papers of Oxford and Cambridge. This linkage grew stronger in the early twentieth century. Between 1916 and 1939, the proportion of Oxbridge entrants to these senior grades rose from 80 to 90%, while, in contrast, a tutor from Leeds University told the McDonnell Commission in 1913 that 'among the class of parents from whom our students are drawn, the possibility of entering the civil service is at present very little known' (Lowe, 1985). The result was that, for most of the twentieth century, the most prestigious departments of state, such as the Foreign Office, continued to draw heavily, if not exclusively, on the ancient universities. By the start of the twentieth century, it was virtually impossible to aspire to a senior position in the church, the public schools, the civil service or the law without having first been at Oxbridge, which, as Harold Perkin (1989, p. 87) has shown, became 'the main articulator of the social ideal of the professional class'.

The establishment of Appointments Boards at Oxford in 1892 and Cambridge in 1901 marked the start of a sustained attempt to locate graduates in posts in industry. It was to prove a remarkably successful initiative. By 1913, 20% of Oxford graduates were finding their way into industry and from Cambridge 'of the order of two or three hundred a year' (Sanderson, 1972, pp. 52–4). But one key indicator of social trends here is the observation, made by both Sanderson and Perkin, that, year by year, more Oxbridge students were being recruited from families with business backgrounds than were leaving to enter industry (see Sanderson, 1972, p. 54). The two leading universities were providing a 'genteel' education for the sons of successful industrialists which opened up career routes beyond those of the family concern, at exactly the same time that it was establishing direct links with industry. Even more significantly, most of these graduate recruits to industry had degrees with no immediate or obvious applicability to industry. As Sanderson (1972, pp. 58–9) has pointed out:

> From the civic universities industry demanded scientists and technologists, men with specific skills that could be directly applied to production or research. . . . At Cambridge before 1914, however, industry recruited arts graduates from the beginning. . . . They believed that there was a strong connection between high academic ability and business success . . . a clear reflection and imitation of the civil service.

It was this trend that led to the highest echelons of significant parts of British industry being colonized by men with a liberal education rather than a scientific or technological background for much of the twentieth century. It may help to explain some of the prevalent attitudes within industry, not least to higher education itself.

But it was the development of university teaching as a career which led to the professions rather than industry being seen as the natural target of the young graduate. The late nineteenth-century growth of Oxford and Cambridge opened up the possibility of a lifetime spent within the university. As Sheldon Rothblatt (1968, p. 246) has pointed out, the decline of private tutoring coincided with the emergence of a new type of don, professionally interested in scholarship and using his (it was almost exclusively a masculine profession at this time) influence as teacher to form the character of his students by passing on a set of values which incorporated a respect for learning for its own sake. At the moment that the new northern civic colleges were recognized as universities, they sought staff who could confirm their arrival on the academic scene. In some cases the results were spectacular. At Liverpool by 1894, of 18 professors only 4 were not recruited from the two ancient universities. Elsewhere the situation was similar (Lowe, 1985, p. 155). A system of patronage developed in which leading members of the old universities saw it as part of their duty to ensure that the right people got the top jobs in the new 'Redbrick' universities. Henry Sigwick and his friend James Bryce discussed in their correspondence who should be given the principalship of both Birmingham University and Owens College, Manchester at the turn of the century (Lowe, 1987, pp. 173–4).

This determination to appear academically respectable resulted in the transformation of these Redbrick universities at the start of the century, from local colleges making a real attempt to service their local industries into institutions which emphasized the importance of the liberal arts. In the process, there was a shift away from providing part-time courses, many of whose students were young workers in local industrial and commercial concerns, towards full-time provision over 3 years of more markedly academic courses. When the Yorkshire College at Leeds first attempted to federate with the Victoria University, it was excluded on the grounds that it did not offer a liberal education. The first Vice-Chancellor of Birmingham, Oliver Lodge, spoke of 'the unfortunate impression abroad that Birmingham either does not possess or does not encourage a Faculty of Arts' (Jarausch, 1983, p. 53). Under his leadership, that faculty trebled in size in 12 years. So sharply was this felt in the locality that by 1911 a local ratepayers' association was complaining that Birmingham University

> is of no use whatever to the industrial classes; as far as we can see all that has been done by the merging of Mason's Science College into the University has been to divert the funds intended for . . . the industrial classes to the use of the wealthy' (Jarausch, 1983, pp. 53–4).

So keen were these new universities to model themselves on Oxbridge that, in almost all cases, efforts were made to develop a 'campus' or at least collegiate style buildings redolent of traditional collegiate architecture (Lowe, 1982).

If the new Redbrick universities were not to provide the technological education so cherished by the growing urban labour force, where was it to be found? The answer lay increasingly in new technical colleges, which, at the very moment that the civic universities turned away, met this need through a dramatic expansion of the capacity for part-time evening work. Between 1901 and 1911, the numbers enrolled in part-time science and technical classes rose from less than 100 000 to over 700 000 (Jarausch, 1983, p. 49). Much of this work was carried out in new technical colleges set up by local authorities. This was the third major element in the new system that emerged at the turn of the century, acting as a safety valve which allowed the civic universities to develop in accordance with their own perceptions of academic merit rather than in response to the changing needs of their localities. The system was hierarchical, and was soon perceived to be so. The tradition of part-time preparation for industry in a local technical college persisted, and still has vestigial effects. By 1931, only 8000 students from a cohort of over one million were studying full-time in technical colleges: in that year, the Clerk Report discovered no wish from either industrialists or educationalists to see this tradition of part-time work modified (Jarausch, 1983, p. 47). Further, the bulk of entrants were from elementary schools, having left school at 14 years of age. It is little wonder that technical education struggled to establish clear routes to managerial positions for much of the twentieth century in England.

The template which was set up in this way at the turn of the twentieth century has been of critical importance for the interlinking of higher education and industry, and indeed for the survival of a set of attitudes towards higher education which help explain what has come to be known as 'the English disease'. Once established, these attitudes have proved difficult to unseat and have helped to predetermine more recent outcomes. The two world wars forced a much closer liaison between higher education and industry, with the chemical industry being a particular beneficiary of university expertise in the First World War, and the establishment of the Department of Scientific and Industrial Research (DSIR) marking a clear and enduring governmental commitment to the sponsorship of technology and science. Similarly, the development of radar and atomic energy were the most spectacular direct outcomes of the interlinking of industry and the universities during the Second World War. But the post-war expansion of higher education has borne all the marks of its longer-term inheritance rather than of lessons learned at these moments of national crisis.

The characteristic of the post-war era which might have led to a reversal of these historic trends was the tendency for the expansion of higher education to be planned at governmental level, rather than being the result of private and predominantly local initiatives, as had been the case previously. But much of this planning was for separate sectors within higher education, the University Grants Committee (UGC) taking responsibility for the universities, and, immediately after the war, the new National Advisory Council on Education in Industry and Commerce (NACEIC) focusing on technological qualifications. Hardly surprisingly, the two organizations took off in different directions. In 1946, the Barlow Report called for at least one new university 'which would give to the present generation the opportunity of leaving to posterity a monument of its culture' (Stewart, 1989, p. 47). The outcome was not, as might have been expected, a technological university, but Keele, modelled on the liberal arts college, and making no reference to the economic needs of North Staffordshire beyond a strong commitment to the social sciences which some thought would enable graduates to play a leading role in the strong trade union movement of the area. Despite the intentions of the UGC to promote technology within the universities, Keele was to become a model for the later new universities, as the preceived need to reconcile the 'two cultures' dominated debate on university developments. It is true that by the early 1960s the UGC had succeeded in lifting the proportions of pure and applied science students within the universities to 25 and 35% respectively, but the earmarking of less than 2% of the total recurrent grand during the 1950s meant that the universities were largely free to respond to student demand as they saw fit. The consequent emphasis on arts, pure science and social science (accounting for 68% of all students in 1962), was a clear reflection to the historical pattern (Stewart, 1989, pp. 110–11).

Meanwhile, under the aegis of the NACEIC and spurred on by the 1956 White Paper on *Technical Education*, plans were laid for local and regional colleges, working alongside designated colleges of advanced technology, which were to be the main providers of a refurbished higher education for industry. Technological qualifications, below degree level in status, were to be overseen by the National Council for Technological Awards (soon to be popularly known as the Hives Committee). It is in this inheritance from the late nineteenth century that we see the origins of our present binary system, and of sectors of higher education with significant contrasts between them in their perceived linkages with the world of industry and commerce.

The dramatic expansion of the 1960s saw this historical divide being reworked rather than abandoned. In 1963, the Robbins Report established the principle that higher education should be available to all who were qualified and wished to benefit from it. One survey conducted by the Robbins Committee found that undergraduates in applied science subjects were far less well qualified at 'A' level than their counterparts in the pure sciences (Stewart, 1989, pp. 108–109). Accordingly, the Robbins Report proposed both expansion and upgrading for applied science within the university sector: the outcome was the promotion of 10 Colleges of Advanced Technology to full university status. Immediately, these institutions saw the route to academic respectability as being through a process very similar to that which had occurred in the Redbrick universities at the start of the century. During the late 1960s, the universities in general, and these new technological universities in particular, were responsible for a dramatic increase in the number of students taking degrees in the social sciences (particularly economics, sociology and business studies) which far outstripped the growth in applied sciences (Stewart, 1989, p. 110). This reflected a contemporary view that the manpower needs of the wealth-producing sectors of the economy needed more than mere technologists, which in some ways echoed the arguments deployed to justify an increase in the number of arts students at the start of the century.

Meanwhile, the redesignation of the Hives Committee as the Council for National Academic Awards (CNAA: another proposal of the Robbins Committee) opened the door for an implementation of the Robbins principle which would be affordable and which sustained the British tradition of expansion of higher education for industry and commerce through a divided system. With the CNAA empowered to award degrees, and civil servants running scared at the likely cost implications of putting an ever-increasing number of institutions on the UGC list, the announcement in the spring of 1965 of a 'binary policy' led to the recognition of 30 colleges of technology as 'polytechnics' in 1970. It meant that the Robbins proposal for five Special Institutions of Scientific and Technological Research was to be shelved, as was the planning of yet more new universities. As Anthony Crosland, Minister of State for Education, emphasized in his famous Woolwich speech, 'We infinitely prefer [the dual pattern] to the alternative concept of the unitary system' (Stewart, 1989, p. 138). Those institutions most closely concerned with the training and preparation of the industrial workforce were to remain locally funded and within the public sector.

One final irony is the extent to which, once they had begun work, the polytechnics experienced an 'academic drift' that was strangely reminiscent of those that had occurred at an earlier period in other new institutions. In the 1970s, the temptation to mop up student demand which was not met elsewhere, together with considerations of academic respectability, led to a sudden upturn in the numbers enrolled on arts and social science courses. With the 'flight from science' of the early 1970s, even the universities were finding difficulty in filling places on applied science courses, while other curricular areas were heavily over-subscribed. History repeated itself: institutional diversification went along with a scramble for academic prestige which led directly to curricular similarity. Such a development could only recur in a society within which, as Martin Weiner has eloquently argued, deep-seated cultural norms repeatedly block the challenge of entrepreneurship:

> This pattern of behaviour traces back in large measure to the cultural absorption of the middle classes into a quasi-aristocratic elite, which nurtured both the rustic and nostalgic myth of an 'English way of life' and the transfer of interest and energies away from the creation of wealth (Weiner, 1985, p. 154).

It remains to be seen whether what I have described as a peculiarly English historical phenomenon continues to exert influence in the dramatically transformed situation of the late twentieth century. The evidence of tighter governmental control and planning of the universities during the 1980s appears at this remove to be ambiguous, if not at times self-contradictory. On the one hand, some of the universities of technology with the best records of placing graduates in industry were among those which suffered most in the round of cuts announced in July 1981: on the other, the same round of cuts, and much recent policy, has sought to confirm the position of technology and applied sciences within the universities. There is clear evidence of more direct industrial and commercial involvement in planning the provision made by universities. Barclays Bank have endowed a chair in management information systems at Warwick University, and the Institute of Directors have funded a chair in business studies at the same university. The chair in marketing at Lancaster University is funded by the Institute of Marketing. This pattern of direct industrial sponsorship is matched within the polytechnic sector: the professorship of estate management at Oxford Polytechnic, which is funded by an estate agency, is but one of several similar initiatives (Shilling, 1989, p. 39; see also Kogan and Kogan, 1983). It may be that the imperative that the present government is placing on both universities and polytechnics to seek external sources of funding may result in an increasing blurring of the binary divide and may make the historical pattern I have described here a thing of the past. A growing similarity in patterns of funding, and the foreseeable merging of university and polytechnic funding agencies, would certainly work towards this end. Or is the English caste system in higher education, which has resulted in, at best, an arm's length relationship with industry and commerce, particularly on the part of the most prestigious institutions, so deeply rooted that it will re-emerge in whatever administrative structure is set up during the 1990s? The evidence of the most recent 100 years does not give grounds for unbridled optimism.

References

Jarausch, K. H. (ed.) (1983). *The Transformation of Higher Learning, 1860–1930*. London: Routledge and Kegan Paul.

Kogan, M. and Kogan, D. (1983). *The Attack on Higher Education*. London: Kogan Page.

Lowe, R. (1982). Building the ivory tower: The social functions of late nineteenth century collegiate architecture. *Studies in Higher Education*, **7**(2), 81–91.

Lowe, R. (1985). English elite education in the late nineteenth and early twentieth centuries. In Conze, W. and Kocha, J. (eds), *Bildungsbergertum im 19. Jahrhundert*, Vol. 1, pp. 147–62. Stuttgart: Klett Kotta.

Lowe, R. (1987). Structural change in English higher education, 1870–1920. In Muller, D. K., Ringer, F. and Simon, B. (eds), *The Rise of the Modern Educational System: Structural Change and Social Reproduction, 1870–1920*, pp. 163–78. Cambridge: Cambridge University Press.

Perkin, H. (1989). *The Rise of Professional Society: England since 1880*. London: Routledge.

Rothblatt, S. (1968). *The Revolution of the Dons*. Cambridge: Cambridge University Press.

Sanderson, M. (1972). *The Universities and British Industry, 1850–1970*. London: Routledge and Kegan Paul.

Shilling, C. (1989). *Schooling for Work in Capitalist Britain*. Lewes: Falmer Press.

Stewart, W. A. C. (1989). *Higher Education in Post-war Britain*. London: Macmillan.

Weiner, M. J. (1985). *English Culture and the Decline of the Industrial Spirit, 1850–1980*. Harmondsworth: Penguin.

Wright, P. (1989). Access or exclusion? Some comments on the history and future prospects of continuing education in England. *Studies in Higher Education*, **14**(1), 23–40.

3

Thinking about Science and Practice in British Education: The Victorian Roots of a Modern Dichotomy

Robert F. Bud and Gerrylynn K. Roberts

Given that scientific research is expensive and that technological innovation is remunerative, what is the connection between them and how can it be enhanced? The question is now seen to be more than merely a matter of administration. Recent critics of British culture (Weiner, 1981; Barnett, 1986) have conflated two indictments: British economic decline and the culture's attitudes to technology and industry. In supporting these arguments, the anti-industrial tenor even of scientific education is often cited. The status of pure science is seen to be an indication of the greater power of those who despise industry. However, our analysis suggests that this equation of pure science with opposition to industry is misleading.

Historically, the relationship between science and technology has been tackled by means of case studies of particular innovations in the distant and in the recent past (Gibbons, 1984, pp. 96–116). However, neither the application of chemical theory to the development of synthetic dyes, nor the development of the atomic bomb, should alone determine our view of the structure of science. Our approach has been the opposite. Instead of taking selected cases of technical developments, we have studied the concepts and visions that underlie thinking about science and technology in Britain and are a crucial part of British culture. This approach has highlighted the central role of educational issues in the definition of the widely used model of separate but related pure and applied science, which has been dominant for more than a century. The model of curiosity-based pure science throwing up results that could be separately applied has had such strong appeal that it sometimes seems obvious. But 100 years ago, questions about the relations between science and technology were seen to be of immediate importance not in terms of research funding, but as an educational problem. All Western countries faced the challenge of training people for new industrial societies, drawing upon public science and private technical skills, esoteric knowledge and traditional craft skills. Pure and applied science are not natural phenomena, but are phrases that were coined at the same time and were part of the same process.

In modern 'high-tech' society, historians across Europe and America are looking anew at the historical origins of concepts inherited from the last century (Krohn *et al.*, 1978, pp. vii–x). They have found fundamental differences in the institutional and cultural solutions found in different countries. National differences are particularly striking in the case of the teaching of technology, and have attracted considerable attention. In France, the prestigious educational institutions established after the Revolution, such as the École Polytechnique, were essentially concerned with science-based professional training (Weisz, 1983; Sebastik, 1983). A vision of applied science developed at the École Centrale was known as *la science industrielle* (Weiss, 1982). In Germany, development of the Technische Hochschulen as educational centres separate from the universities, and the consequent need to identify their domain, led to analogous visions of an autonomous science-based technology. In both France and Germany, there was a well-established engineering professionalism that provided vehicles for this conception (Manegold, 1978, pp. 137–58). Similarly, in America, the growth of scientific engineering was part of the legitimation of the professional engineer as against the mere mechanic (Calvert, 1967, pp. 63–106; Reynolds, 1986). Thus in all these countries, technology as a separate body of knowledge reflected the separate identity of the engineer and his training. In Britain, the education of the engineer was formalized much later than on the Continent. A scientific basis for engineering was seen to be less significant to the definition of the British engineer's skill (Weingart, 1978, pp. 251–86). It is also evident, from report after report, that British manufacturers were loath to see the factory reduced to a laboratory with their secret processes exploited as public knowledge (Society of Arts, 1853). In each of these countries, the need for such education and status led to particular formal relationships to the sciences. In Germany, of course, the humanistic tradition of *Wissenschaft* and *Bildung* had established knowledge as a good thing in itself (Ben-David, 1971). The French positivist tradition, too, located truth in an objective science.

Science did not come to be structured and defined just through the influence of thinkers: complex institutional and professional factors underlay the process of its definition. In Britain, science and technology were promoted vigorously by entrepreneurial civil servants, scientists, politicians and industrialists. Just as on the Continent, their relative power and interests were expressed through the definition of science (Turner, 1978, pp. 356–76). Critics of British education have seen the Victorian legacy as an aspect of the weakness of the 'industrial spirit' (Weiner, 1981). The history of chemistry in the nineteenth century shows that, on the contrary, the system resulted at least in part from industrialists' reasoned pressures.

For most practitioners, chemistry was the biggest of the nineteenth-century sciences and it was the science most readily recognized as 'useful'. Ironically, chemistry was so obviously promoted for utilitarian ends and yet it became the pure science *par excellence*. In both Sweden and Germany, chemistry provided the model of the split between pure and applied science in the eighteenth century. Separate and distinct arguments were made for its incorporation into the university curriculum as the basis of useful innovations in metallurgy on the one hand, and as part of natural philosophy on the other (Meinel, 1981, pp. 366–89; 1985, pp. 25–45; 1988, pp. 89–115). Britain had a rather different academic structure; the attempt to organize and structure chemistry there contributed to the patterning of British science as a whole in the nineteenth century.

The notion of a scientific discipline includes the dual function of transmitting and creating knowledge. It is thus striking that the traditional accounts have analysed the formation of the discipline of chemistry in Victorian Britain principally in relation to the emergence of a research tradition. The eloquent rhetoric of research surrounding the establishment of the important chemical schools from the 1840s and the ethos of research emanating from the Chemical Society (founded in 1841) tend to reinforce this view. The spirited promotion of research by interested parties before the famous parliamentary enquiries some three decades later lends it further support. We would like to suggest that the formation of the chemical discipline in Britain in the nineteenth century should *not* be seen primarily as the result of a drive to establish a research tradition. Instead, we argue that the important sector for establishing the discipline was the activity complementary to research – teaching and the purposes which it ought to serve. The notion of 'pure science' was conceived initially as a category of teaching, rather than as a separate activity. And at the same time a complementary category of applied science was defined. Applied science acquired two different meanings: one connotes the application of pure science, the other an enterprise in its own right, often today called technology.

In practical terms, the crucial difference in Britain was between teaching science as general knowledge which can be of intrinsic benefit and can also be applied on the one hand, and, on the other, teaching science as part of systematic practical training towards a particular vocational end. We have called the former the 'science college' model and the latter the 'polytechnic'. This distinction is not merely philosophical or retrospective. It was hammered out in the course of urgent educational debates during the nineteenth century. Embodied at the time in bricks and mortar, chairs, curricula and regulations, this dichotomy still has resonances in today's attempts to mould a society geared to high technology. Neither of these ideas reflect antagonism to science or technology, nor to manufacturing industry. Both counted among their prophets leading industrialists and men of state as well as scientists.

We can follow the emerging distinction through the debates over the form of a central scientific school in London. An early forerunner was the Royal College of Chemistry. The principal motivation for the establishment of this, the first of the new wave of chemical schools in the 1840s, was a disire to train practical chemists rather than researchers. Medicine, including pharmacy, agriculture and a wide range of chemically based manufacturers were the anticipated beneficiaries of the new institution. In order to appeal to as many practical interests as possible, both among financial backers and potential students, a universal curriculum was promulgated. Formally, it was based on the German university model as developed by Justus Liebig at Giessen. However, it was also extremely *practical* in a manner that would be acceptable in England. The curriculum rested on the teaching of the principles of chemistry by means of training in general analytical methods in the laboratory. No training related to any specific technical area was included, but advanced students were to be taught research methods through the study of analysis. A student so instructed, the argument ran, would be well prepared to function in any applied chemical environment. This stress on the training of the mind through the study of general principles, served to make chemistry a suitable subject within the traditional English liberal education. At the same time as it could be argued to satisfy the requirements of chemical practitioners, the curriculum could also fulfil the research goals of the academics administering it by training future academic researchers. In the hands of the academics, then, chemistry as a discipline became an abstract scientific subject, separate from the various areas of practice from which it had emerged. On this model, 'liberal' *scientific* training was the basis of what we may call 'higher' technical education in England.

It is perhaps surprising that any single metropolitan institution could have such an influence in British education, especially one which failed financially. However, since it was scientifically a success, great attempts were made to put the Royal College of Chemistry on a sound footing by means of government funding. It was thus caught up in the major national debates over the government support of British education and its advocates extended that debate to the support of science in general. From the 1850s, there was an attempt to create a highly centralized system on the French model. Two famous parliamentary enquiries of the 1860s and 1870s were largely concerned with this issue. Witnesses before them developed two models of scientific education which still inform educational thinking today. It is these that we have called the 'polytechnic' model after the French École Polytechnique, which attempted to provide an education in technology, and the 'science college' model in the British university tradition, according to which science would be taught as the liberal basis for the subsequent development of specialist technological expertise in the workplace.

These educational debates took place against a background of British industrial power highlighted by the Great Exhibition of 1851. At the same time, the seeds of decay already seemed to be visible to Prince Albert and his friends. They diagnosed poor technical education in Britain in contrast with the elaborate system established in France. The solution seemed to be to import that system. During the early 1850s, French-style institutions were promoted by a new government Department of Science and Art, but with little success. Often cited was the example of the École Centrale des Arts et des Manufactures in Paris. Especially intended for aspiring manufacturers, this institution was animated by the concept of *la science industrielle*, expressing unity in a curriculum that stretched from abstract theory to particular applications. In Britain, this model came in the long run to be complementary to that of the 'science college'.

In London, some tried to re-portray the already established, state-supported School of Mines as a 'polytechnic' model institution (devoted in this case to a single technology, an analogue of continental mining schools) because the original 'science college' vision of that institution had not prospered. Founded by the government in 1851 as the School of Mines and of Science Applied to the Arts, this institution was designed to offer training, by means of laboratory work, in the general principles of all the basic sciences, plus training in the scientific principles of certain applied subjects. Mining was meant to be the first in the latter category. The School was intended to spawn a number of offspring applied institutions around the country which would concentrate on locally relevant subjects. It 'saved' the Royal College of Chemistry by absorbing it as its own chemistry department. A change of director in the mid-1850s focused it more narrowly on mining. In 1861, after much internal wrangling, its remit as a mining school was confirmed by a Treasury Committee of enquiry. This was much to the distaste of the non-geological scientific professoriate there, which had favoured the broader 'science college' model. Another example of a French-style 'polytechnic', again devoted to a single area of technology, appeared in 1864 when the Royal School of Naval Architecture, financed by the Admiralty, and administered by the Science and Art Department, opened in South Kensington. It was explicitly modelled on the École Impériale du Génie Maritime in Paris. The course began with a thorough grounding in pure and applied mathematics, and then proceeded to the theory of practice (including practical work) of various aspects of shipbuilding and marine engine design. It also included study of the principles, with laboratory work, of the basic sciences of physics, chemistry and metallurgy. Significantly, students were meant to spend only 6 months of each of their 3 years on course work at South Kensington; the remainder of the time was to be spent actually at work under supervision in a shipyard. To the modern eye, this is immediately recognizable as equivalent to the sandwich course.

Appealing as this may have seemed and vigorous as its promoters were, this type of education did not get the support of manufacturers. An investigation by the Royal Society of Arts on the subject of technical education for workmen had already made clear the employers' view that what should be taught was the science on which industries were based. Applications, they argued, could only be learned through actual practice in the workshop. This was to be an enduring view reinforced by a dual worry: first, that training in actual techniques might lead to the loss of trade secrets; and, secondly, that were training given in a state-supported workshop (another possibility canvassed), it might lead to unfair state-subsidized competition with private enterprise (Society of Arts, 1853). Neither were skilled workers enthusiastic for a vocational education that they feared would be narrow and socially limiting. They also supported the 'scientific' model of technical training. This was, after all, what had been offered piecemeal by many Mechanics' Institutions (Samuelson Committee, App. 19, p. 474). So the technical education offered to artisans at 'secondary' level turned out to be consistent with the model of higher technical education promoted by scientists.

During the late 1860s, the 'polytechnic' conception of such institutions as the South Kensington School of Naval Architecture and the School of Mines, lost out in turn to the 'science college' ideal. This was not due solely to manufacturers' and artisans' scepticism; in fact, the educational and political climates in which science functioned had changed. There was political concern about the three areas of education in which the state was involved: elementary education, technical education and teacher training. During the re-evaluation of political issues following the Second Reform Act of 1867, attempts were made to bring these three areas into one system. Now, there arose a new demand – the training of teachers of science. Academics realized that they could make a case to do that job.

Following an unsuccessful opposition attempt in the early summer of 1867 to promote an elementary education Bill, the new Conservative Government put forward its own measures. The civil servant at the head of the Department of Science and Art, Henry Cole, drafted a comprehensive scheme for the Government's consideration (Samuelson Committee, App. 12, pp. 459–61). This scheme united 'primary or elementary education' with 'secondary or technical instruction' and with higher education, including scientific instruction for future teachers and manufacturers. At almost the same time, Bernhard Samuelson, iron manufacturer and reforming Liberal MP, reported to the Government the details of a personal survey of continental technical education and submitted his own proposals. They were very like Cole's, although they were arrived at through an analysis of the needs of industry rather than via educational imperatives. For Samuelson, the teaching of science as the substance of technical education was the answer. To achieve this, better teachers were a prerequisite, and training them should be the responsibility of the Government. He argued for a system which would send the best elementary school pupils on to science classes run all over the country via the Department of Science and Art and, from there, to the School of Mines in London or to local colleges to receive advanced education which would fit them to be teachers. At the same time, these local colleges could also train future manufacturers (*Industrial Progress* 1867–68). In Cole's scheme, it was intended that there should be at least four such science colleges linked to local industry in the provinces, in addition to the School of Mines and the Royal College of Science in Dublin.

Samuelson chaired a Parliamentary Select Committee whose report in 1868 echoed his and Cole's schemes. It called for a thoroughgoing reform of the education system into an integrated progression that would satisfy the needs of workmen, foremen and managers. Most urgently, children destined to be workmen needed elementary education. Lack of this made it impossible for them to take advantage of the available adult artisan classes. The Committee also recommended a reorganization of middle-class secondary schools to include more science. In the same category, it suggested that some of the so-called endowed schools, then also under investigation, should be reconstituted as 'science schools' with close links to their local industries. At the top of the hierarchy, there would be regional colleges with a national central institution in London. Such colleges, the Committee argued, could not be run on fees alone, but would require support from some combination of the State, local interests, private endowments, and maybe even local property taxes. The

Committee was clear that such colleges would have the greatest impact if established in centres of industry 'because the choice of such centres tends to promote the combination of science with practice on the part of both the professors and pupils' (Samuelson Committee, p. ix).

The Samuelson Committee pointed to a major implication of its own report – the need for a dramatic expansion of the teaching profession. So in this report we can see the emphasis of technical education shifting from working-class education for the artisan to middle-class education for the teacher, the manager and the proprietor. The Committee stressed that the virtue of the system was that the required expansion of the teaching profession could be achieved by the same institutions which trained the others. Cole's thinking was clearly to the fore. It is hardly surprising that, among the Committee's practical suggestions, was the possibility that the School of Mines in London might prove useful as a general science college and that further investigation of the complex government scientific establishment in South Kensington, including the land-locked School of Naval Architecture, was needed.

Some 6 months after this report, a new Liberal Government came to power. William Forster, the new minister with responsibility for education (now most associated with bringing in compulsory schooling), made clear that he wanted to establish a new teacher training school as soon as possible and also to review the whole system of education, including scientific and technical education (House of Commons, 3 *Hansard* 198, 19 July 1868, cols 161–2). Instead of implementing the elaborate, and expensive, institutional reforms of the Samuelson Committee, in 1870, he set up the now famous Devonshire Commission on Scientific Instruction and the Advancement of Science. Linking in its very title the teaching of science with research, the Devonshire Commission showed that there had been a change in emphasis among science educators. In its first report, published in March 1871, the Commission recommended merger of the three government science-teaching institutions (the Royal College of Chemistry, the Royal School of Mines and the School of Naval Architecture) to form a science college for teachers in a new building rising in South Kensington (Devonshire Commission, vol. 1, pp. vii–viii). The recommendation was confirmed by later reports covering teacher training and science teaching in the schools.

This recommendation was not, however, to be easily implemented. The charge of state competition with private enterprise was a major challenge faced by all those in favour of the scheme for a state-funded science college in South Kensington. Alexander Williamson, Professor of Chemistry at the then privately funded University College, put the case forcefully to the Devonshire Commission in his tellingly titled lecture, 'A Plea for Pure Science' (Devonshire Commission, vol. 1, qq. 1190, 1204; Williamson, 1870). He argued that prospective students would select a state-supported institution preferentially with a view to obtaining government posts. Williamson was particularly perturbed that the South Kensington project had been undertaken without consulting the scientific community outside government institutions. He in fact had been active in getting teaching included on the agenda of the Devonshire

Commission precisely because of this. Additionally, Williamson expressed influential views about the relationship of teaching and research at university level. Adamant that academe was no place to learn the applications of science, he argued in a by-now traditional manner, that that was best done in the real-life situation of the works *after* a solid foundation of scientific principles. The one vocation for which academe could offer effective training was teaching, for the university actually was a 'works' where teaching was concerned. Indeed, many of his former pupils had become successful teachers. The obvious conclusion was that no special training institutions were needed either for future industrialists or for future teachers. The university already did the job. As regards research, Williamson was equally firm. This too was to be the function of the academic. Thus, though against state support, Williamson supported the rationale behind the science college model.

Indeed, it was to be 10 years before the Government's Normal School of Science and Royal School of Mines officially opened in South Kensington. In that time, another inquiry, the confusingly entitled Samuelson Commission concerned with applied science, was held. This time, the focus was the training not of teachers, but of engineers and managers in industry, the appliers of science. Yet, the conclusions of the Devonshire Commission provided a model; the results were complementary. Just as a state-funded school for training teachers was set up as an eventual outcome of the Devonshire Commission, the establishment of the Central Technical Institution, intended as a 'polytechnic' and explicitly dedicated to applied science, was ratified by the Samuelson Commission. Both located in London, on opposite sides of the same road in South Kensington, the existence of the two institutions rested on the assumption that pure science was the basis for future applications. So, however parochial the debates concerning the setting up of these specific institutions were, the arguments they sustained were of more general importance and subsequent significance for British scientific education.

Therefore, we can see that the concept of pure science was very powerful – it underpinned both the dominant educational models. The Samuelson Committee had suggested a dual role for tertiary education: training applied scientists and training teachers. The Devonshire Commission shifted the balance to the teachers. Thereby pure science, as the professional education of teachers and as the universal basis of education for all technical professions, was confirmed as the principal focus of the curriculum. The conclusions of the Devonshire Commission ratified what had been evolving since the 1840s in the case of chemistry: pure chemistry was put at the head of a hierarchy of knowledge. Firmly in control of what constituted appropriate knowledge for the whole of the chemical community were the academics, rather than representatives of the practising community. In conclusion, in the mid-nineteenth century, promoters of two types of institution, the 'polytechnic' and the 'science college', jostled for influence. Implicit in each form was a model of the relation between pure and applied science. In the 'polytechnic', the two were closely linked. In the 'science college', as the idea was progressively defined, pure science was the principal business of academe, as the training of teachers and as the universal basis for practical training outside. It is perhaps not surprising that, in the subsequent century of academic expansion, the 'science college' model remained attractive to professors of such subjects as chemistry. The educationally conceived relations between pure and applied science became, for a time, generalized truths.

Today, a century after the Victorian commissions, their arguments are echoed in current debates. This chapter has suggested a note of caution to those who would point to the British interest in pure science as an indicator of disdain for industry. Instead, we suggest that the notion of pure science was constructed in the nineteenth century precisely so that a practical scientific education could be publicly provided in a way acceptable and useful to private industry. The UGC's 1988 draft report on 'The Future of University Chemistry' cited industrial testimony such as 'although it is useful for graduates to have some insight into vocational aspects of chemistry, courses should not be diluted with excessive amounts of applied chemistry' (Stone, 1988, p. 29). From a good deal of such evidence it concluded that '. . . teaching at an advanced level is best achieved in a thriving and dynamic research environment' (Stone, 1988, p. 4). Equally, the arguments for the Victorian 'polytechnic' model have been deployed in recent years to support innovations such as those fostered by the Manpower Services Commission (now the Training Agency), whose centralizing role itself echoes the Department of Science and Art. Debates over central funding of the Information Technology Colleges (ITECs), City Technology Colleges (CTCs) and the Technical and Vocational Education Initiatives (TVEI) would have amused Henry Cole.

Bibliographical Note

For fuller documentation, see R. F. Bud and G. K. Roberts, *Science versus Practice: Chemistry in Victorian Britain* (Manchester: Manchester University Press, 1984). For further background to our argument, see D. S. L. Cardwell, *The Organisation of Science in England* (London: Heinemann, 1957; 1972); S. F. Cotgrove, *Technical Education and Social Change* (London: George Allen and Unwin, 1958); E. T. Layton, Mirror-image twins: The communities of science and technology in nineteenth-century America, *Technology and Culture*, **12**, 564–80 (1971); Roy MacLeod, Scientific and technical education, in G. Sutherland (ed.), *Education, Government and Society in Britain: Commentaries on British Parliamentary Papers*, pp. 195–233 (Dublin: Irish University Press); P. W. Musgrave, *Society and Education in England since 1800* (London: Methuen, 1968).

References

Barnett, C. (1986). *Audit of War: The Illusion and Reality of Britain as a Great Nation.* London: Macmillan.
Ben-David, J. (1971). *The Scientist's Role in Society: A Comparative Study.* Englewood Cliffs, N. J.: Prentice-Hall.

Calvert, M. A. (1967). *The Mechanical Engineer in America, 1830–1910*: Professional Cultures in Conflict. Baltimore: Johns Hopkins University Press.

[Devonshire Commission]. *Reports of the Commissioners Appointed to Make Inquiry with regard to Scientific Instruction and the Advancement of Science, and to Inquire What Aid there is Derived from Grants Voted by Parliament, or from Endowments Belonging to the Several Universities of Great Britain and Ireland and the Colleges Thereof, and Whether Such Aid could be Rendered in a Manner More Effectual for the Purpose.* Vol. 1: *First, Supplementary, and Second Reports, with Minutes of Evidence, Appendices, and Analyses of Evidence*, P.P. 1872 (536) XXV.1.

Gibbons, M. (1984). Is science industrially relevant? The interaction between science and technology. In Gibbons, M. and Gummett, P., *Science, Technology and Society Today*. Manchester: Manchester University Press.

House of Commons, 3 *Hansard* 198, 19 July 1868, cols 161–2.

Industrial Progress and the Education of the Industrial Classes in France, Switzerland, Germany etc., P.P. 1867–68 (13) LIV.67.

Krohn, W., Layton, E. T. and Weingart, P. (eds) (1978). *Sociology of Sciences Yearbook: The Dynamics of Science and Technology*: Dordrecht: D. Reidel.

Manegold, K.-H. (1978). Technology academised: Education and training of the engineer in the 19th century. In Krohn, W., Layton, E. T. and Weingart, P. (eds), *Sociology of Sciences Yearbook: The Dynamics of Science and Technology* (Dordrecht: D. Reidel), pp. 137–50.

Meinel, C. (1981). 'De Praestantia et utilitate Chemiae'. Selbstdarstellung einer jungen Disziplin im Spiegel ihres programmatischen Schrifttums. *Sudhoffs Archiv*, **65**, 366–89.

Meinel, C. (1985). Reine und angewandte Chemie: Die Entstehung einer neuen Wissenschaftskonzeption in der Chemie der Aufklärung. *Berichte zur Wissenschaftsgeschichte*, **8**, 25–45.

Meinel, C. (1988). *Artibus Academicis Inserenda*: Chemistry's place in eighteenth and early nineteenth century universities. *History of Universities*, **7**, 89–115.

Reynolds, T. S. (1986). Defining professional boundaries: Chemical engineering in the early 20th century. *Technology and Culture*, **27**, 694–716.

[Samuelson Commission]. *Royal Commission on Technical Instruction, First Report*, P.P. 1884, XXVII.9; *Second Report with Appendices, etc.*, P.P. 1884, XXIX.73; P.P. 1884, XXX.1; P.P. 1884, XXI.1; P.P. 1884, XXXI (I), 9; P.P. 1884, XXXI (I), 555.

[Samuelson Committee]. *Report from the Select Committee on Scientific Instruction for the Industrial Classes together with the Proceedings of the Committee, Minutes of Evidence, and Appendix*, P.P. 1867–68 (432 and 432-I) XV.1.

Sebastik, J. (1983). The rise of technological science. *History and Technology*, **1**, 25–43.

Society of Arts (1853). *Report of the Committee Appointed by the Council of the Society of Arts to Inquire into the Subject of Industrial Instruction with the Evidence on which the Report is Founded*. London: Longman.

Stone, F. G. A. (1988). *Report of the Chemistry Review: The Future of University Chemistry*. Ms final draft copy.

Turner, F. M. (1978). The Victorian conflict between science and religion: A professional dimension. *Isis*, **69**, 356–76.

Weiner, M. J. (1981). *English Culture and the Decline of the Industrial Spirit, 1850–1980*. London: Hutchinson.

Weingart, P. (1978). The relation between science and technology – a sociological explanation. In Krohn, W., Layton, E. T. and Weingart, P. (eds), *Sociology of Sciences Yearbook: The Dynamics of Science and Technology*, (Dordrecht: D. Reidel), pp. 251–86.

Weiss, J. H. (1982). *The Making of Technological Man: The Social Origins of French Engineering Education.* Cambridge, Mass.: MIT Press.

Weisz, G. (1983). *The Emergence of Modern Universities in France 1863–1914.* Princeton: Princeton University Press.

Williamson, A. W. (1870). *A Plea for Pure Science, being the Inaugural Lecture at the Opening of the Faculty of Science in University College London.* London: Taylor and Francis.

Part 2

Public and Private Funding

4

Industry Contributions to Higher Education Funding and their Effects*

Gareth Williams and Cari Loder

Background

Until the 1980s, finance was not a significant management or policy issue in higher education. Although there were important differences in the funding of universities and non-university institutions, they were similar in that a high proportion of the total came from a single source, the University Grants Committee (UGC) in the case of the universities and the Advanced Further Education Pool, subsequently regulated by the National Advisory Body, in the case of the polytechnics and colleges. It was expected by both the suppliers and users of funds that this core funding would be sufficient to maintain the financial and academic integrity of the institutions. Any funding over and above the basic core grants was treated as 'soft money' that did not really enter into university or polytechnic accounts. Staff employed on this 'soft money' were rarely treated as full members of their institutions. For most of them, a research contract or other fixed-term appointment was essentially an apprenticeship or waiting period before obtaining a permanent academic appointment. Financial management in universities and polytechnics was geared mainly to allocating resources and regulating expenditure and not to the generation of income. There was little concern with costing or pricing. If a proposed initiative was deemed to be worthwhile by an appropriate member of the academic staff, and provided it did not impose excessive direct financial costs on the rest of the institution, it was generally undertaken. Many academic staff did private consultancy work, and again, provided it did not make excessive claims on the time available for university or polytechnic work and did not impose direct financial costs on the institution few questions were asked.

A concern of many governments in the 1980s has been to shift some of the

* In part, this chapter summarizes some of the findings of a report to the Department of Trade and Industry and the Council for Industry and Higher Education. We are grateful to the sponsors for their agreement to the use of these extracts. The main report is published under the title *Business Funding of Higher Education* (forthcoming). The views expressed are those of the authors alone.

financial burden of higher education away from the public purse. This is one of the themes of a recent OECD report (Williams, 1990), which reports similar developments in many other Western European countries: 'The first, and most widespread [motivation] is the hope that the private sector can be a source of supplementary funding and thus relieve governments of some of the cost burden.' This attitude is not unnaturally viewed with some suspicion in industry: Malpas (1988) writes: 'In BP we are clear that it is not our purpose to substitute our shareholders' money for the withdrawal of public funds.'

However, it has not been only stringency in public expenditure which has induced higher education to seek funding from business. Nor has saving public money been the only objective of British government policy towards higher education in the 1980s. Many government initiatives have encouraged partnerships more positively through matching grants and similar arrangements. One of the main aims has been to accelerate the development of new technologies and their adoption by British industry. To this end, government programmes have been heavily concentrated in information technology and biotechnology, with some emphasis on other areas of engineering and business studies. There have been government schemes in which the provision of public funds has been dependent, at least in part, on success in obtaining commitments from the private sector to supplement the public funds.

Patterns of industry funding

The proportion of higher education income derived from industry has risen sharply during the 1980s. However, in 1987–8, only 2.8% of the income of universities and 0.9% of that of polytechnics consisted of research contracts from industry. Its distribution is very skewed. Throughout the decade, over 85% of university research income from industry was earned by medical, engineering and science departments. In 1987–8, medical faculties received research income of nearly £30 million from industry, and engineering departments nearly £25 million. In terms of income from industry per member of staff, engineering was dominant with the average academic engineer earning £3200 in 1987–8, that is £1000 more than in the next subject, business and accounting. Another measure of skewness is that in 1987–8, 40% of research income from industry was in five universities.

The above figures refer to research grants and contracts only. The contributions of business to higher education are known to be much wider than this. However, little quantitative information is available about the extent of these other contributions. An attempt was made, therefore, to begin to fill this gap in a study undertaken for the Department of Trade and Industry and the Council for Industry and Higher Education by the Centre for Higher Education Studies.

Tables 4.1 and 4.2 summarize the principal results of that study: 2.4% of the income of polytechnics and 6.3% of the income of universities can be deemed to have originated with 'business'. This amounts to just under £170 million in the case of universities and about £22 million for polytechnics. In total, therefore, the contributions of business to higher education in 1987–8 in the activities identified in Tables 4.1 and 4.2 was about £192 million. This is more than 2.5 times the figure based on research contracts alone. Of the universities' £170 million, just over three-quarters consisted of payment for teaching or research services, with the remaining one-quarter, or £40 million, being some form of donations in cash or kind. Of the £130 million for the purchase of academic services, about £5 million is the gross income (turnover) of companies in which universities have a majority shareholding: the remaining 97% is money earned by the university from other industrial and commercial enterprises. In the polytechnics, all but about 2% (£500,000) was in the form of payments for research and teaching services. Our figures suggest that the total income of polytechnic companies in 1987–8 was very low, and business donations were almost negligible. It is confidently predicted that both these will increase substantially now that they have independent corporate status.

In addition to the figures shown in Tables 4.1 and 4.2 industry and commerce contributed to the costs of about 3500 full-time and part-time university students from home and overseas. If we assume that business paid the fees of these students, then the total expenditure of business on university student sponsorship in 1987–8 would have been about £4 million. There may also have been a contribution to the living expenses of the full-time students, but this has been ignored, partly on the grounds that there is no basis for estimating the contribution to maintenance costs and partly because these are not part of the resources available to higher educational institutions. A proportionate figure for the polytechnics might be about £1 million. It could be argued that the figure should be higher because polytechnics are more directly concerned with vocational courses: it could, however, equally be argued that it should be lower on the grounds that all other categories of business income are much lower in the polytechnics than in the universities. In terms of total industry contributions, the student sponsorship figures are, however, at present small. If they are added to the £192 million derived from Tables 4.1 and 4.2, it suggests that the total business contribution to higher education in 1987–8 was just under £200 million.

This figure excludes any estimate of the individual consultancy earnings of academic staff. The only comprehensive information available is that produced in 1974 by Williams *et al.* Their figures were based on information collected in 1971 and show that, on average, academics added 12.5% to their salaries from outside earnings. If this proportion is applied to the 1987–8 figures, this would amount to about £80 million. However, a substantial part of this is in effect university money that is being 'recycled' through payment for external examining and similar activities. Another substantial proportion is in the form of royalties of various kinds. It is not clear whether this should or should not be considered a 'business earning'. Furthermore, of the straight consultancy earnings, a significant proportion came from government and not from industry. However, even after allowing for all these reservations, there can be little doubt that in comparison with the figures being discussed a substantial amount is being paid by business for the individual consultancy services of members of

Table 4.1 Estimated total income of universities from business, 1987–8

	Total income £(000)	Income from business, £ (000)										Total business income
		Research contracts	Short courses	Other services	Gifts etc.	University companies gross	Trusts	Gifts in kind	Sponsored staff	Seconded staff	Other	
Total	2522 000	76 629	25 782	24 094	17 811	5255	1937	8419	1201	1034	7808	169 973
% distribution of business income		45	15	14	10	3	1	5	1	1	5	100
% of total income		2.83	0.95	0.89	0.66	0.19	0.07	0.31	0.04	0.04	0.29	6.28

Table 4.2 Estimate of business funding of polytechnics, 1987–8

	Total income, £(000)	Income from industry, £(000)								
		Research contracts	Industrial training	Full-cost courses	Polytechnic companies	Cash gifts	Gifts in kind	Sponsored staff	Unpaid lecturers	Total business income
Total (all polytechnics)	743 792 000	8441	2237	10 858	0	26	319	194	35	22 111
% of total income		1	0	1	0	0	0	0	0	2
% of income from industry		38	10	49	0	0	1	1	0	100

Source: *Business Funding of Higher Education*

academic staff. Taking all these considerations into account, a reasonable estimate might be £25 million, giving a gross financial contribution to British higher education in 1987–8 of the order of £225 million, which is just under 7% of its total recurrent income.

There would remain the question of how any figure of private consultancy earnings is to be interpreted in terms of assessing the contribution of business to higher education. From the point of view of business enterprises, payment to individual academics differs little in principle from payment to their departments or universities for the same consultancy services, even though it makes no contribution to institutional funds. However, it may be contributing to staff development: and contacts made may, on occasion, lead to partnerships that are directly advantageous, financially or otherwise, to the academic institution. It certainly is the case also that the possibility of external earnings permits higher education institutions to recruit and retain essential staff.

Overhead charges

It is generally, though not universally, believed in higher education that there is considerable industry money around and the main concern of higher education institutions is to ensure that a reasonable proportion of it helps to support their general academic functions. The issue of overhead payments is, therefore, a major preoccupation of institutional managers and there is widespread acceptance that the issue is not a simple one. In one institution, members of the research team were told that 'The university is really interested in the generation of surpluses so that teaching and academic research can be funded.' In another, 'It is also important to see that full-cost research and consultancy contracts do not damage teaching and research in the university. One way of ensuring this is to make sure that adequate overhead payments are made by the funding bodies.' In another it was admitted that 'we do not have a good record of retrieving overhead costs. However, a significant proportion of the overheads is retained by the departments and, therefore, does not appear as entering general university funds.' Some respondents told us of other ways in which departments receive contributions to 'overheads', e.g. in the form of gifts of equipment. In another university:

> in the past departments have been fairly selective about the research they undertake and it has been argued that research contracts were, in effect, donations towards the departments' own research rather than contract work from outsiders. However, this is changing as a result of new financial circumstances. The recently expanded Industrial Liaison Office has a specific function of encouraging a more disciplined approach to pricing of research and consultancy contracts.

Most finance officers agree, however, that an excessively actuarial approach to overhead charging may be counterproductive and not all overheads can, or necessarily should, find their way into university or polytechnic accounts. We were given numerous examples of intangible benefits and the intricacies of disentangling both the costs and benefits on both sides.

There were similar expressions of concern about the dangers of adopting too narrow an attitude with respect to private consultancy earnings. In one polytechnic, the Dean of Art and Design pointed out that:

> the Faculty has a large proportion of Associate Lecturers who are practising designers, usually with their own firms. They cannot be expected to put their regular work through the polytechnic, particularly since they have their own facilities and are, therefore, not using polytechnic equipment.

In one very research-intensive university we were told that 'academic work always takes precedence over consultancy work, but so long as the consultancy does not take up more than one day a week or constitute more than 50 per cent of salary, permission is usually given'. In another, it was said that 'consultancy work is encouraged as it may well feed back into teaching and may also generate future contracts'.

Another university 'has traditionally adopted a sympathetic attitude to private consultancies for members of staff. There is a strong belief that in many subject areas it is desirable for individuals to have experience outside the university. On the whole, regulation is of time and resources rather than income earned.' We were told of the view of one head of a computing department that 'members of staff were allowed two months private consultancy a year. If any member of staff is unable to double his income during that two months I do not want him in the department.' In other words, anyone who could not command that kind of salary in the marketplace is not of high enough calibre to work in a good university computer science department. Furthermore, students in such a high technology area would expect their staff to have practical, up-to-date, professional experience. In another, very respected scientific and technological institution, we were told that 'consultancy income for individuals is seen as a perk to those staff who can get it. It is seen as an incentive to stay at the college and an inducement to do good research.'

Business funding and staff careers

From the point of view of higher education institutions, the main obstacle to further development of financially rewarding partnerships with industry and commerce is the tensions it imposes on the career structures and aspirations in universities and polytechnics. Until the 1980s, the conventional academic career was based upon appointments with effective lifetime tenure for established academic staff after a relatively short period of probation at the beginning of their careers. There was little pressure on staff with such secure conditions of employment to be active in seeking external funds unless a particular area of activity interested them personally.

Alongside these tenured staff, younger research workers were often recruited to work on specific externally funded activities, usually, but not exclusively, research projects. The conditions of work of these research staff were frequently poor and their job security minimal. However, the attraction was that most of them would be able to find secure academic employment well before they reached the stage of their careers when job mobility becomes difficult.

During the 1980s, three changes have occurred which have disrupted this equilibrium. In the universities, formal tenure was abolished in the 1988 Education Act: few new appointments were made to permanent established posts; and the number of people employed on non-established posts increased very considerably. This underprivileged group of research and other contract staff no longer have the safety valve of the prospect of secure employment within a reasonable period of time. However, they are still treated as if such a possibility exists. It is an almost universally held view of such staff in both universities and polytechnics that, in the words of Crawshaw (1985), 'those employed on contract research have an inferior status compared with academics who are employed on other bases – within the university community they are second class citizens'. Moreover, they often believe they are expected to earn profits in order to keep in work their colleagues with more secure employment contracts. Meanwhile, they themselves are often on extremely short-term contracts with no job security beyond the existing research project or short course programme. Where the funds for their salaries do come from general university funds, staff on fixed-term contracts remain vulnerable in that their contracts have to be renegotiated at frequent intervals. If their colleagues have permanent contracts, this means that the whole burden of any downward adjustment must be borne by those who are less fortunate. The net result is that their conditions of employment are not only worse than their colleagues in established posts but are also considerably worse than their colleagues in similar jobs in the business sector.

During the early and mid-1980s, when there was a tendency for an over-supply of graduates in many areas, universities were able to continue to recruit such staff even though most of them were not satisfied with their conditions of work. In the likely employment conditions of the 1990s, this will not be tolerated. Shortages of graduates in a wide range of disciplines will make it very difficult for universities and polytechnics to recruit people on the casual terms that have so far been widely used. Because the majority of people who have worked on industry-funded projects have had this type of contact, it can be predicted that unless there is radical change in the employment conditions of such staff in both universities and polytechnics, shortages of suitable staff will be the main obstacle from the higher education side to further expansion of higher education–business partnerships during the 1990s.

An evaluation of business contributions to higher education

In evaluating 'business funding' in higher education, it is necessary to distinguish two very closely related ideas: business activities of universities and polytechnics, and the funding they receive from industry and commerce. The latter category can itself be divided into two broad components: purchase of academic services by business enterprises, and unearmarked contributions by business to universities and polytechnics to help them carry out their normal academic activities. One effect of the changes in public funding of higher education in the 1980s, which is likely to accelerate in the 1990s, is that universities and polytechnics are being required to behave more like 'businesses' in all their activities. They are receiving much higher proportions of their income in the form of payments for services rendered rather than in unconditional grants. They are also, however, seeking to increase the amount of funds they obtain from industry and commerce, both in the form of unrestricted gifts and grants and in the form of income from the sale of academic services of various kinds.

There is, in general, a substantial difference between research partnerships and those which are primarily concerned with training and consultancy. This is reflected clearly in two very different kinds of university or polytechnic company. One, which might be called the traditional kind of university company, is concerned mainly with the exploitation of a specific area of research within the university. A generic term for these is 'spin-off companies'. The other kind of academic company, most strongly reflected in the new polytechnic companies that have been organized within the past 12 months but which have also been established in a few universities, are concerned with selling a much broader range of academic services, and the kind of research that is likely to yield patentable results is not a large part of their concern. Their primary purpose is to sell the services of academic staff who are likely to be underworked, or at least underpaid, if they continue to be dependent solely on income from public funds. They have two broad functions: one is to increase the amount of consultancy income, and more specifically consultancy 'profit' available to the institution, and the other is to convert existing private consultancies of academic staff members and informal consultancies of departments, into institutional consultancies from which the university or polytechnic derives some financial benefit.

These considerations lead finally to an examination of two important issues, one technical and one more fundamental. The technical issue is the treatment of income from business funding in the accounts of a university or polytechnic. The fundamental issue is the nature of a university or polytechnic as an academic institution. One extreme view of 'the university' is that it exists in order to teach undergraduate and postgraduate students and to undertake basic research. Any activity which cannot be categorized under one of these headings detracts from its real functions and is justified only if it generates a surplus which can be used to advance teaching and research. Until the 1980s, this was the underlying assumption on which both university and polytechnic accounts were usually based. The income and expenditure of the institution were those general, unrestricted grants from public or private sources which were available for allocation for teaching or research at the discretion of the appropriate decision-making bodies in the academic institution, plus any 'profit' from trading activities. Supplementary activities were treated as self-balancing items that might be undertaken for academic or promotional reasons, or because of the interests of members of the academic staff, but the only part that would appear in university accounts would be any surplus available for general university use.

The alternative view is that the university or polytechnic is an economic enterprise in the knowledge industry, and it is appropriate for it to sell whatever mix of academic services is most cost-effective. Traditionally, there has been no doubt that selling conventional undergraduate and postgraduate courses paid for out of public funds has been the most profitable product; therefore, issues about whether or not it is appropriate to undertake other work have been of marginal significance. Even when universities have used some of their resources to undertake public service activities, such as academic time spent on government advisory committees or providing concerts for the local community, these were usually deemed both marginal and complementary to the central academic activities of the institution.

If, however, it is the case, as it has been during much of the 1980s, that core public funding is insufficient to maintain the existing size and organizational structure of the institution, a university or polytechnic has the choice either of reducing its size until it is viable within existing core resources, or of expanding its income from other sources. In these circumstances, the function of external income, of which business income is an important part, is to help maintain the economic viability and hence the academic integrity of the institution. If a university has the alternative of going bankrupt or of earning external income for consultancy work, then that consultancy is *de facto* part of the core activity of the institution and should be recorded as such in institutional accounts.

The issue is sharpened when academic staff do not have permanent appointments. Is academic integrity best maintained by keeping staff together even if they spend a substantial part of their time on activities that are not strictly academic? Or is the 'idea' of the university more important than the individuals who constitute any actual university, implying that the latter should be shed in order for the university to be able to confine itself to its proper functions of education and basic research? Although rhetoric in some universities tends towards the latter position, the reality is that nearly all academics in practice accept the former even though many believe that it is the job of the government to provide sufficient general funds for it not to be necessary to make the choice. However, there remains, and will always remain in the background, the conceptual question of determining the point at which a university or polytechnic carrying out consultancy services and the like becomes in reality a consultancy enterprise that also provides some training. Conversely, at what stage does competition from chartered universities or statutorily incorporated polytechnics with large inputs from public funds become unfair with respect to other partnerships and limited companies operating in similar areas?

For the time being, these remain 'academic' questions. The main part of the income of all higher education institutions is still explicitly devoted to traditional teaching and research. However, it is a question that might be asked of some departments of medicine, engineering and business studies. At what stage does their commercial involvement make it appropriate or beneficial to them, to leave the university altogether? Moreover, if new arrangements for student fees and bidding for funds for undergraduate and postgraduate teaching and research result in serious loss of financial resources in some institutions through price-cutting by competitors, these institutions will inevitably be driven to increase their income from other sources. This is not necessarily damaging. Indeed, one of the strengths of 'the European University' is its capacity to adapt to changing circumstances. However, it is necessary to be aware that fundamental change is taking place and that it may have very profound consequences for the nature of academic institutions.

Henry Wasser (1990), writing from the perspective of the USA and several continental European countries, is in no doubt that a sea change is taking place:

> Obviously the university as a long-lived institution has survived by constantly adjusting to changing social and political needs. Yet the present rapid and radical move to a university adaptive in a major fashion to economic development, to an entrepreneurial university, would appear to go beyond modification to a sufficiently changed structure that no longer for many institutions fits the time-honoured definition of a university.

Many observers claim that traditional humanities and social sciences disciplines are in serious danger. Williams (1990) refers to the emergence of a 'vulnerable sector, areas of teaching and research which not only lack adequate resources but which are deserted by top quality students and staff'. Two important policy questions are whether this is, in fact, occurring to any significant extent; and if it is, whether it matters. Crawshaw (1985) asks whether private sponsors are ever likely to be convinced that the study of obscure ancient languages is worth their support? If support is not forthcoming, does this mean that these areas are not academically worthy of study?

The alternative view is that the polytechnic, or university, is a holding company with a variety of different 'divisions' and the income and expenditure of each, whether it be associated company, or running the refectory, or the university press, are all part of that enterprise. This is the practice in the USA and is one reason why comparisons of income and expenditure between Britain and the USA are extremely difficult.

Just as universities in the nineteenth and early twentieth centuries adapted to the need to prepare people for employment in the Civil Service and liberal professions, so the higher education of the late twentieth century needs to adapt, and is adapting, to the need to promote, and to prepare people for, the high-technology, information-rich society of the twenty-first century. Viewed in these terms, partnerships between universities and business enterprises are analogous to links between university medical schools and teaching hospitals, or between professional associations and specialist departments in universities and polytechnics. Funding from business for applied research or consulting or specific training courses, becomes simply another source of institutional funding, neither better nor worse than that received for undergraduate courses or pure research. But it might be damaging if government decides that its funding also is to be determined solely on market criteria.

References

Crawshaw, B. (1985). Contract research, the university and the academic. *Higher Education*, **14**, 665–81.

Malpas, R. (1988). Suitor or bride. *Times Higher Educational Supplement*, 2 September.

Wasser, H. (1990). Changes in the European university: From traditional to entrepreneurial. *Higher Education Quarterly*, **44**(2) (Spring 1990).

Williams, G. L., Blackstone, T. A. V. and Metcalf, D. (1974). *The Academic Labour Market*. Amsterdam: Elsevier.

Williams, G. L. (1990). *Changing Patterns of Finance in Higher Education*. Paris: OECD.

5

The 'US Model' for Higher Education: Structure and Finance

Keith Tribe

The USA had 9 726 168 students enrolled in public higher education institutions in the autumn of 1986; in the UK the figure was 945 000.[1]* Looked at another way, there were more public higher education students enrolled that year in Texas, which at the time had a population of 16 685 000, than in the entire polytechnic and college HE sector in the UK.[2] Figure 5.1 shows how US enrolments had already passed present UK student numbers by the late 1920s; but what is also evident is the great expansion of student demand in the 1960s and 1970s, reflecting as in Europe the proportionate increase of 18–20-year-olds in the population as a whole.

The USA is, of course, a bigger and wealthier country than the UK – its population is four times that of the UK, while gross national product (GNP) per capita is around half that again of the UK. Any social and economic comparison between the two countries has to take account of these basic facts, even before questions are raised about statistical definitions and the structural features of the systems under comparison. From the figures cited above, we seem able to confirm a general perception that US citizens have a greater rate of participation in post-school education than that of UK citizens; there are also many more institutions of higher education, 3406 in 1986 to be exact.[3] If we added to these figures statistics of degrees conferred, the percentage of the population with higher qualifications, and the financial resources of the system as a whole, we would simply reinforce an initial impression of a higher educational system both more extensive and wealthy than that in the UK.

Not only is the system more wealthy, it is broadly divided between a publicly supported sector of state colleges and universities, and a private system whose income derives from a mixture of private endowments, student fees and contractual income. This aspect, when combined with the sheer size and scope of the system as a whole, provides us with the broad outlines of the 'US model' for higher education – a high participation rate in a differentiated system funded

---

*Superscript numerals refer to numbered notes at the end of the chapter.

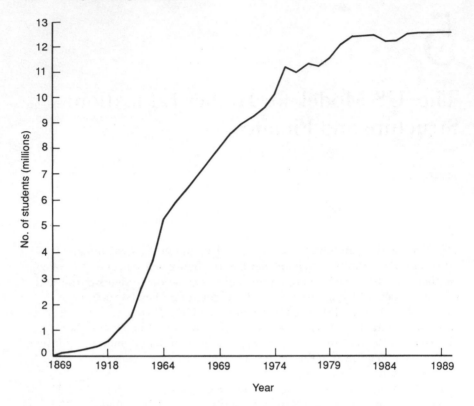

Figure 5.1   Higher education students in the USA, 1869–1990.

by a mixture of public and private money. For European policy-makers concerned with the social exclusiveness and state-dependence of their higher educational institutions, this model seems to have many attractive features. Unfortunately for them, however, this 'US model' is a mixture of myth and mirage. Closer examination of US higher education in the late 1980s discloses a system that shares many of the problems confronting European systems. Furthermore, its institutional and financial structure is not after all so very different from that which has developed in Britain and Europe – except, of course, that it is far richer.[4]

This chapter can do little more than present an outline of the development and current structure of US institutions of higher education. As with the UK, there is no single authoritative account of the evolution of the university and college system, but there are a number of sources from which a general picture can be built up.[5] A recent DES Report is also available, which provides some basic information on the system, although this has to be used with care.[6] The account provided here will focus on two main issues: the financial resources available for higher education, and the distribution of students between types of institution.

One of the more striking features of the US higher education system is the distinction between public and private institutions. This is a historical distinction, in that the development of higher educational provision during the late nineteenth century was facilitated both by the endowment of private institutions, and the establishment of state universities and colleges under provisions dating from the Morrill Land Act of 1862. This Act provided for the endowment of educational institutions out of central funds distributed to states on the basis of their population, and in many cases state administrations met a major proportion of their running costs as well. In this way, major institutions grew up in the public sector whose resources matched or exceeded many of the better-endowed private colleges.

These new state foundations took their place alongside the older-established colleges which had, up to the 1860s, based their teaching almost entirely on a classical curriculum. In the post-bellum period, a 'modern' curriculum became the norm for established and new institutions, both public and private alike. Major new universities were privately endowed from the 1870s to the 1890s, such as Johns Hopkins, Chicago and Stanford. These and other institutions were the beneficiaries of substantial private fortunes; compared with the funding of British university colleges at this time, the private resources available for educational purposes remain breathtaking.[7] During the first three decades of the twentieth century, the practice of individual philanthropy – so important for new private institutions – was replaced by the more organized activities of the Carnegie Corporation and the Rockefeller Foundation. Philanthropic foundations, disposing as they did of substantial resources for research and institutional development, played a major role in determining the shape of the US university system, deliberately concentrating their resources on a few key institutions in both the state and private sectors. Unlike the British system, in which the development of university institutions during the inter-war period presupposed broad comparability of teaching and qualification across institutions, the US system has evolved as one differentiated by level and quality. It is important to note, however, that this process is one that overrides the public/private distinction – or, to put it another way, range and variability in educational level is common to both public and private sectors.

The pattern of public support for higher education also requires some clarification. The public/private distinction arose in the first place because state universities and colleges appeared alongside existing private institutions. In the course of time, however, additional federal funding has been made available which has itself had the effect of blurring the distinction between public and private sectors. Federal funding for higher education has always been indirect – institutions have received funds as the consequence of distinct programmes of special provision, rather than in their own right. The rationale for this is that in this way direct funding would be quickly followed by central control – as, of course, happened in Britain, whose private university system was increasingly subject to government control from the 1920s onwards.

Federal expenditure flows into public and private higher education institutions alike. This is because it is distributed through programmes designed to strengthen research in particular areas in the national interest, assure equal access to post-secondary education for disadvantaged groups, provide vocational training in key occupations, and provide special benefits to special classes of persons such as war veterans and the handicapped.[8] Thus the Servicemen's Readjustment Act of 1944 provided for college-level education for war veterans, as did the Korean War GI Bill of 1952; and the National Defense Act (1958) provided for graduate fellowships and subsidized loans to under-graduates.

It is in funds channelled to individuals that expenditures have been growing most rapidly in the last 20 years – over the period 1968–77, almost $6 billion of the $7 billion added to federal higher education appropriations can be at-tributed to the extension of access financing, in which ex-servicemen and the poor are beneficiaries.[9] In addition to this there is, of course, the funding of research programmes by government departments, the largest spender of which is the Department of Health with $4 billion, followed by the Department of Energy with $2.2 billion out of a total federal research budget of $10.5 billion.[10]

Apart from these direct expenditures by central government, the ability for households to make deductions for children in full-time education, and for individuals and corporations to deduct charitable contributions from their taxable incomes, meant that in 1977 the Treasury received approximately $3.8 billion less than it would otherwise have received if such provisions had not existed. While the former involves a transfer to households with dependants in higher education irrespective of institutional status, the latter charitable and philanthropic flow of funds naturally focuses on selected institutions. Typically, of course, the wealthier private universities will tend to have a roll of wealthy alumni whose contributions are cumulative; hence the $1.8 billion that flowed into higher education from alumni in 1985–6 would almost by definition have gone to the wealthier institutions.[11] Some of these are in the public sector, which derives 4% of its revenue from this source: the HMI noted in their survey that Rutgers and George Mason, both public universities, were making successful efforts to raise income from private endowments and contributions.[12]

Figures 5.2 and 5.3 give a general representation of the overall institutional funding structure. The major difference between the public and private system is evidently in the relative shares of tuition fees and direct government funding; nevertheless, it is also apparent that even the private sector as a whole derives almost 20% of its direct funding from public sources. As might be anticipated, the level of endowment and other private income also differs between the two sectors – but here again attention should be drawn to the fact that such direct individual and corporate funding only represents 14.6% of private sector revenue as a whole. On the basis of these aggregate figures, we can provisionally conclude that the funding structure for the US public sector is not so dissimilar to that prevailing in the UK, while the private sector is distinguished chiefly as such by the high proportion of revenue derived from tuition fees.

There is, however, a problem here, associated with the manner in which the federal government funds higher education. A proportion of the cash flowing into public and private sectors as tuition fees originates with state and federal

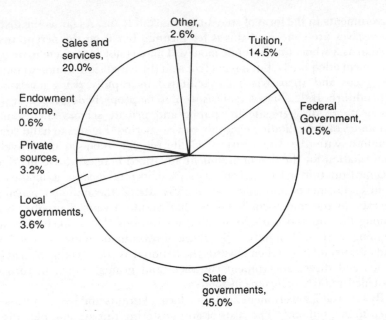

Figure 5.2 Sources of current-fund revenue for public institutions of higher education, 1985–6 (total revenues = $65 billion).

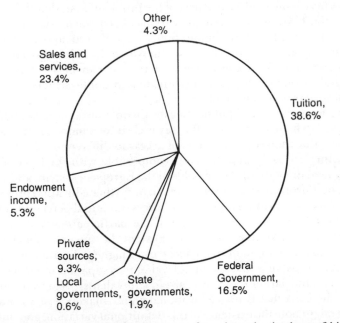

Figure 5.3 Sources of current-fund revenue for private institutions of higher education, 1985–6 (total revenues = $35.4 billion).

governments in the form of student grants and loans. As far as the institutions themselves are concerned this is fee income, but from the perspective of the system as a whole this is public money. There is not space here to develop this argument adequately, but it is evident that the expansion of student numbers in the 1960s and 1970s has been facilitated by rapidly rising levels of public expenditure. If this line of analysis were to be properly developed, it would be necessary to disaggregate the public and private sectors and examine the dynamics of their funding over this 20-year period. Figures to hand comparing Stanford with the University of California for 1969–70 do provide some confirmation for the line of argument advanced here: at this time, Stanford's income from tuition fees was only 23.25% of its total income, as against 20.46% from endowments and gifts, i.e. slightly above the national private sector average in the mid-1980s.[13] Given that Stanford ranked number 6 in 1986 among the top 100 property-holding institutions,[14] it is likely that with the ongoing increase in numbers the share of revenue deriving from endowments and gifts would have fallen towards the national average, compensated by a rise in fee and direct government contracts and grants, which in turn already provided 43.66% of income in 1969–70.

By late 1986, government aid in the form of grants and loans to students had risen to $15 billion.[15] The costs of administering this system, plus the default rates and problems of individual indebtedness, naturally present opponents of recent UK student loan proposals with ready-made arguments against changes to the present UK funding structure. Quite apart from this debate, however, the emphasis here is on a different aspect of the problem: first, that the expansion of access in the USA over the last 30 years has been chiefly sustained by public funds; and, secondly, these public funds have flowed into both public and private sectors alike because of the way in which the federal government funds higher education. As a consequence of this, it can be doubted whether a meaningful distinction between the private and public sectors on the basis of financial structures can be made.

Setting to one side the public/private distinction as a meaningful way of appraising US higher education, the way is clear for a more direct assessment of the higher education sector in terms of access to different levels of study. Very broadly, the US bachelor's degree is comparable with the level of academic work engaged in by 16- to 18-year-olds in the European system, and so properly belongs, by European standards, to school or further education provision. This classificatory qualification immediately alters our initial perception of the sheer size of the US system – for the scale of the participation rates noted in the introductory remarks above is to a great extent the outcome of including levels of educational provision not treated as part of higher education in Europe. We should note in passing that the high level of participation in formal academic education on the part of 16- to 18-year-old equivalents[16] represents an achievement for the USA that British educational policy-makers wish to emulate. But while we might note the existence of this definitional variation, and duly observe its significance for the structure of educational provision as a whole, the objective of this chapter is to identify the leading features of US higher education at levels comparable with what would be considered higher education in a European context. Defining our objective in this way excludes a significant proportion of the student numbers contained in Fig. 5.1, and once adjustments are made in this way the US figures for participation in higher education programmes begin to look more like those prevailing in some European countries.

Before we move directly to distinguish institutions of higher education according to level of educational provision, some additional remarks can be made about overall participation rates in US higher education, as well as age-specific rates. There are a number of complex issues here; our conclusions can only be very provisional, since they indicate the need for detailed data on the social and regional composition of age cohorts, as well as details of ages of entry by type of institution and duration of study. As with any form of demographic data, the distinction between the absolute size of any given age cohort in the population, and the percentage rate of participation of that group in HE, must be constantly borne in mind.

Quite evidently, part of the rise in student numbers entering higher education during the late 1960s and the 1970s can simply be attributed to the proportionate increase of the relevant age groups within the population as a whole. Figure 5.4

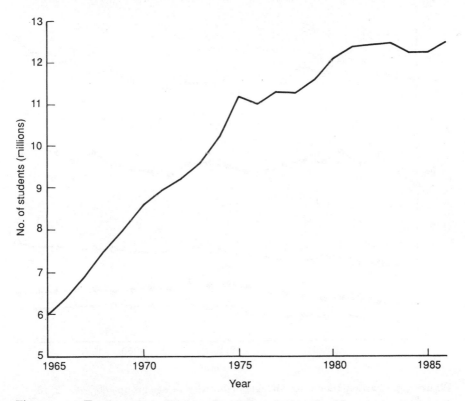

Figure 5.4   Total number of higher education students 1965–86.

focuses on the total student numbers in the period for which we also have data on the relevant age cohorts.

Once the time-series is presented in this way, it becomes clear that there was a continuously steep rise in numbers from 1965 to 1975, at which breakpoint the student population had almost doubled. It then continued on a more slowly rising trend. This increase is a compound of rising numbers and a rising participation rate; the question is, which is the more important contributory factor? Any discussion of age-specific access has, of course, to allow for the distortions of the demographic roller-coaster as bulges and troughs pass through the population. In the UK, we have seen a mid-1980s peak in the 18- to 19-year-old age group, and educational institutions and employers are by now aware of the falling trend in this age-range of the population in the 1990s.[17] In the USA, this peak came somewhat earlier, with 4.3 million 18-year-olds in 1979 projected to fall to just under 3.2 million in 1992.[18] Educational institutions are always subject to fluctuations in demand brought about by demographic factors; but of greater interest to reformers is the age-specific rate of participation.

This is shown in Fig. 5.5, which presents age-specific participation rates over

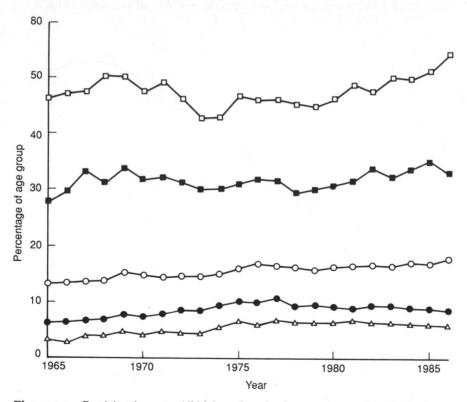

Figure 5.5   Participation rate: All higher education by age group 1965–86. □, 18–19 years; ■, 20–21 years; ○, 22–24 years; ●, 25–29 years; △, 30–34 years.

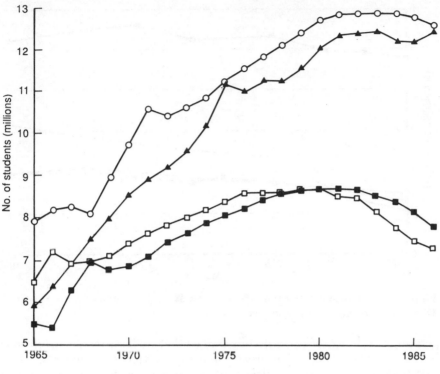

Figure 5.6   Higher education population against total cohorts, 1965–86. □, 18–19 years; ■, 20–21 years; ○, 22–24 years; ▲, total students.

the period 1965–86. What is immediately striking here is the general stability of existing rates, with some important minor fluctuations. The implication is clearly that the massive rise in student numbers over the period 1965–80 is primarily the result of a rise in the number of younger people in the population at large, and not the result of greater pro-rata access.[19] This general conclusion is confirmed by Fig. 5.6, which shows the curves for overall cohort numbers alongside the total student population already presented in Fig. 5.4.

'Average' stable participation would be denoted by each cohort tracking the total student number notably, those aged 18–21 fall away from the trend, whereas the 22- to 24-year-olds do follow the student curve. If Fig. 5.7 is consulted, we then find that in fact that numbers of under-22s have declined in the HE system during the 1980s, whereas those over 22 years of age have increased.[20]

Funding access for these increased levels of demand was certainly an achievement for the USA, but it is sobering that the considerable expenditures involved have not radically altered overall participation rates. Figure 5.5 does, on the other hand, reveal the high levels of participation in higher education by

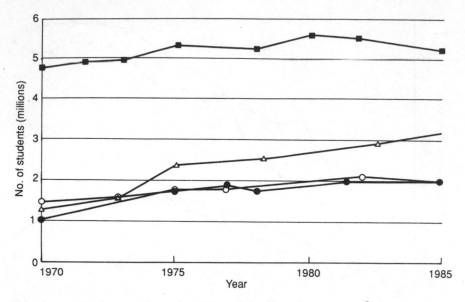

Figure 5.7   Student enrolment by age, 1970–85. ■, under 22 years; ○, 22–24 years; ●, 25–29 years; △, 30 years and over.

persons over the age of 22 – reflecting the fact that students remain in full-time higher education longer than usual for British degree-level students,[21] that part-time study is more prevalent, and that it is easier for older students to re-enter the educational cycle. In fact, as can be seen from Fig. 5.7, it is only among the older age groups that demand has consistently and significantly risen throughout the 1980s.

Once more, then, we find that, on closer inspection, precisely those features of the US system that have been talked up as exemplars for British developments turn out to be either chimerical or inimitable. First, the US government has over the past 20 years committed ever-increasing sums to higher education to maintain – not to increase dramatically – existing rates of participation of the relevant age-groups.[22] Secondly, the most significant rise in demand for higher education, independent of demographic fluctuations, comes from the over 30s. Quite how this demand is distributed throughout higher education is not immediately evident, but it is clear that institutional and financial barriers for re-entry into higher education are not so great in the USA as they are in Britain. Going down this road in Britain would not be cheap; i.e. not cheap for a government as this is where much of the funding to facilitate this access comes from in the USA.

There is a great deal more that needs to be said about these problems, for they raise complex issues and once more data needs to be disaggregated so that the dynamic factors governing broad trends can be identified. For the moment we will have to be satisfied with this indication of the broad trends, and pass on to the final aspect of the US system that is to be discussed here, the distribution of students between institutions of varying levels and type. Here again, even at the very broad aggregative level at which we are working, some interesting conclusions can be drawn.

So far, there has been only indirect reference to the structure of educational provision in US higher education. Figures 5.8 and 5.9 reveal that not only are there more than twice as many students in the public sector as in the private, but in both sectors students are clearly differentiated by type of institution.

The actual distribution of students between type of institution is, however, of greater relevance here. The 2-year colleges offer associate degrees, and the 4-year colleges associate and bachelor's degrees; universities offer bachelor's (undergraduate) and higher (graduate) degrees. There is a marked preponderance of students in public higher education at the lowest level, whereas in private institutions it is the 4-year institutions that account for the largest share of students. The trend over time is of interest too: in both the public and private sectors, university enrolments have remained relatively stable, whereas there have been marked variations both upwards and downwards for the 2- and 4-year institutions.

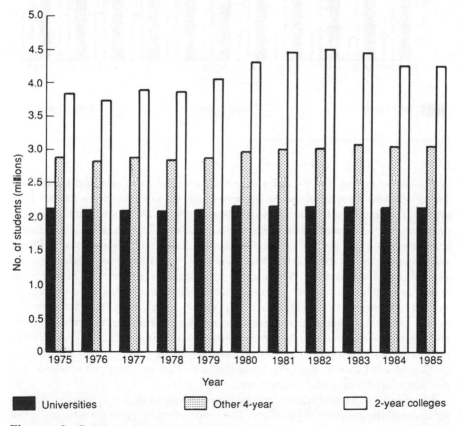

Figure 5.8 Public student enrolments in the USA, 1975–85.

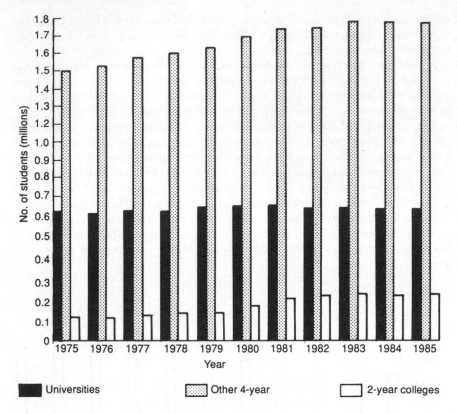

Figure 5.9   Private student enrolments in the USA, 1975–85.

Broadly speaking, the 2- and 4-year colleges offer associate and bachelor's degrees that in Europe would be accepted as a qualification for entrance to a first-degree course only. For all institutions, only 17.6% of students gaining a degree in 1985–6 were awarded master's or doctor's degrees, which covers the level of study equivalent to European universities and polytechnics.[23] There are, of course, major qualitative variations between institutions, rendering easy generalization impossible. Whereas the UK operates a system of higher education in which the quality of degree-level work is monitored by a process of external examining and validation, the assumption being that an approximately equal standard is maintained for movement between courses of study and into the labour market, this does not operate at any level in the USA. Within subject areas, doctoral theses can vary enormously in quality, while the general quality of educational delivery at bachelor's level in the private sector for instance can also be widely discrepant.

The distribution of students into institutions has to be set alongside the age structure of the students themselves. The preponderance, and growth, of 2-year colleges in the public sector points to a greater adaptability of this lowest level of the US system, for it is here that older persons without post-secondary education can most easily enter the system, either part- or full-time. This is not a level comparable with European higher education systems, but it illustrates the greater degree of flexibility in the US system. On the other hand, this could be a temporary trend if the duration of stay of younger entrants is rising and thus rendering such access redundant. Broadly speaking, as more of the population becomes certified, we might expect that mature educational participation was conducted as training within firms by employers.

The US higher education system is not only organized in a different way from that of European higher education, it is more market-oriented in that courses and institutions vary widely in rigour and quality. The direct costs per student for degrees also vary widely, both within and between the public and private sectors.[24] Taken together, these and other aspects of the US system of higher education make it difficult to draw definitive conclusions on a comparative basis. It has been argued in the foregoing that no unambiguous 'US model' can be constructed as an exemplar for educational policy-makers in the UK. There is certainly a greater degree of access to a system differentiated by quality of provision as well as by type of certification. But a great deal of this is to do with a different approach to the management of transitions between compulsory and voluntary educational provision from that prevailing in the UK. If there is one clear lesson that can be drawn from an examination of the US education system, it is that educational policy should be directed to an educational system as a whole, rather than tinkering with various levels in an unco-ordinated way as has been the case in the UK during the 1980s.

The 'American way' has always been to mobilize vast resources to achieve social and economic objectives, in the process creating a great deal of waste and disorder; this is the way of the market mechanism, and it is evident in both the strengths and weaknesses of US higher education as outlined above. On the other hand, the USA is also a highly bureaucratized nation, which is, for example, why the educational statistics available are of a much higher quality than those for the UK. Whatever the US system achieves is the outcome of a complex interaction of market and bureaucracy over a period of decades. If any aspect of the US system is to be emulated in the 1990s, then it cannot be done by following the 'American way', however attractive its outcomes might be. The dynamic properties of the US system cannot be acquired simply by importing some of the features of a complex structure. In any case, the level of resources deployed in the US higher education system during the twentieth century has never been available in the UK, and never will be. If serious changes to our educational system are to be effected at this point in time, they have to take proper account of the nature of the forces that have shaped the system that we at present possess. Only in the light of a balanced assessment of such forces can meaningful reforms be made. And given the lack of large-scale resources, to be effective these reforms will have to be carefully planned and co-ordinated.

This is, of course, not typical of present policy. The interest that has recently been shown in the US system of higher education is a symptom of our problem, not its solution. Lacking a proper understanding of the strengths of the UK system, it is too easy to argue for the wholesale introduction of elements of a (poorly understood) foreign system as a means of replicating US performance. There is a real danger that, in attempting such wholesale innovation, the real strengths of the UK higher education system will be cast aside. For there are real strengths in the UK system, where we enjoy a comparative advantage with respect to institutions within the European Community. Perhaps the chief benefit of considering the structure of contemporary US higher education is to redirect our attention to more general problems of higher education in contemporary industrial societies.

Notes

1. National Center for Education Statistics (1988). *Digest of Education Statistics 1988*, Table 131, p. 153. Washington, D.C.: US Department of Education. Department of Education and Science (1989). *Statistical Bulletin 4/89*, Table 1. London: HMSO. The UK figure includes both part- and full-time students enrolled in higher education courses, as does the US figure.
2. A total of 685 544 in Texas, 523 200 in the UK.
3. National Center for Education Statistics (1988). *Digest of Education Statistics 1988*, Table 5, p. 12. Washington, D.C.: US Department of Education.
4. It is striking that consolidated up-to-date information on the UK state education system is scattered in a number of publications of varying accessibility and quality, whereas the US government publishes a comprehensive annual digest of educational data from pre-school provision to continuing education for the private and public sectors alike. The only problem in the UK is actually gaining access to recent US Government publications; the sole nominated deposit collection in the LSE Library (BLPES), but delivery and cataloguing are at present years behind.
5. A recent overview can be found in M. Trow (1989). American higher education – past, present and future. *Studies in Higher Education*, **14**, 5–22.
6. HMI (1989). *Aspects of Higher Education in the United States of America*. London: HMSO. This was reported in the *Financial Times* under the headline 'Education "must copy US College system"' (31 May 1989, p. 12). Since the Report is a DES publication, the Inspectorate implicitly compares UK polytechnics and colleges with the US system as a whole. Despite the allowances that have therefore to be made, its view that the performance of the US higher education system is not so different to that of the UK and is in many respects notably inferior coincides with the arguments advanced here. The *FT*'s version was presumably based upon a DES press release that reflected politically motivated aspirations rather than the views of the HMI as expressed in their report.
7. For an outline of this, see K. Tribe (1990). The accumulation of cultural capital: The funding of UK higher education in the twentieth century. *Higher Education Quarterly*, **14**, 20–34.
8. C. E. Finn (1978). *Scholars, Dollars and Bureaucrats*, p. 8. Washington, D.C.: Brookings Institution.
9. C. E. Finn (1978). *Scholars, Dollars and Bureaucrats*, pp. 11–12. Washington, D.C.: Brookings Institution. Appropriations under the Higher Education Programme for 1988 were set at $11 billion, of which $5.32 billion was earmarked for student financial assistance, $2.63 billion for guaranteed student loans and $1 billion for

tuition assistance for military personnel (*Digest of Education Statistics 1988*, Table 257, p. 300).

10. National Center for Education Statistics (1988). *Digest of Education Statistics 1988*, Table 257, p. 302. Washington, D.C.: US Department of Education.

11. National Center for Education Statistics (1988). *Digest of Education Statistics 1988*, Table 227 p. 262. Washington, D.C.: US Department of Education. Total voluntary support in 1985–6 was $7.4 billion; contributions from alumni represent the largest single category, followed by transfers from non-alumni individuals ($1.78 billion) and from corporations ($1.7 billion). For an estimate of federal tax expenditures, see E. R. Sunley (1978). Federal and state tax policies. In D. W. Breneman and C. E. Finn (eds), *Public Policy and Private Higher Education*, p. 284. Washington, D.C.: Brookings Institution.

12. HMI (1989). *Aspects of Higher Education in the United States of America*, p. 5. London: HMSO.

13. Calculations made by E. Hutchinson on the basis of Stanford's *Annual Financial Report 1970–71*, in The origins of the UGC. *Minerva*, **13**, 613.

14. The market value of its endowment at the end of fiscal year 1986 was $1.26 billion (*Digest of Education Statistics 1988*, Table 248, p. 282). Because this is by definition wealth accumulated over a long period, it can reasonably be supposed that expansion in the scale of activities of the university would be financed by the rise in share of contributions from students.

15. R. Musgrave (1989). Buddy, can you spare $50,000? *The Guardian*, 5 December, p. 21.

16. That is, since what we would treat as 16–18-year-old schooling is in the USA supplied by autonomous college institutions, access to this level of educational provision is facilitated for older age groups.

17. What the DES failed to note in the early 1980s was that this general population movement was not typical for those social strata actually producing students entering degree-level studies. Variations in the birth rate are not only time-specific, but vary at the same time between social classes. The situation may well be reversed in the USA (see below).

18. US Bureau of the Census data presented as Fig. 1-1 in D. W. Breneman and C. E. Finn (1978). An uncertain future. In D. W. Breneman and C. E. Finn (eds), *Public Policy and Private Higher Education*, p. 4. Washington, D. C.: Brookings Institution.

19. This participation rate is a crude measure of HE students against total population. This measure distorts the picture, as only certain sections of the population engage significantly in higher education. However, if we were to refine our measure to take account of this, we would then need to take account of a number of other factors, such as age of entry, the relation of part-time to full-time study, the duration of courses and of periods of study. This would take us beyond the preliminary assessment attempted here.

20. Here we need to know whether students are staying on in the system longer (possibly on an increasingly part-time basis), or whether they are entering later.

21. The median age for gaining a doctorate was 33.5 years in 1985–6, the physical sciences conferring degrees on the youngest group at a median of 29.9 years, education on the oldest at 39.4 years. National Center for Education Statistics (1988). *Digest of Education Statistics 1988*, Table 208, p. 243. Washington, D.C.: US Department of Education.

22. These generalizations need to be decomposed by social class, analogously with the

remarks made above concerning the UK. If this were done, the conclusions reached here could well require modification.

23. Out of 1 830 000 degrees conferred, 288 567 were master's and 33 653 doctoral degrees. National Center for Education Statistics (1988). *Digest of Education Statistics 1988*, Table 140, p. 163. Washington, D.C.: US Department of Education.

24. Duc-Le To (1987). *Estimating the Cost of a Bachelor's Degree: An Institutional Cost Analysis*, p. 15. Washington, D.C.: Office of Educational Research and Improvement, US Department of Education.

Part 3

Graduates and the Needs of
Employment

6

Graduates of Higher Education: What do Employers Expect in the 1990s?

Peter Meyer-Dohm

The challenge of the 1990s for industry and commerce

Prognoses for the 1990s are as numerous as the recommendations based on the catalogues of demands which industry and commerce have to take account of if they want to survive the last decade of this century and emerge safely into the next millennium. At the same time, a large number of authors and institutes have made it their business to produce profiles of the 'Manager 2000'. One thing is certain: the number of these forecasts and their variety is a mark of the inscrutability of the future and of the multitude of options which it offers.

All forecasts are united on one point at least – the future will bring with it profound changes, probably accompanied by upheavals and symptoms of crisis, which are to be seen as the expression of a far-reaching alteration of the framework conditions of economic activity in Europe. Further, it is believed that an acceleration of change has already been observable for some time, which can therefore be extrapolated for the coming decade.

Alongside this general tenor of prognoses, there is a series of fields on which agreement exists. I shall briefly sketch the five challenges facing companies in the future which are relevant to our topic:

1. Competition will increase for the industries of the European nations, not only as a result of the completion of the Single Market, but also because isolation of this market from the rest of the world does not appear possible. One need only refer in this context to the competition from Asia and its continuing attempts to secure a foothold in Europe. Even those industries and commercial enterprises which are not directly in the mainstream of international competition can expect far-reaching consequences from this development.
2. The role of the customers and their demands will in future become yet more significant. This applies not only to the price/performance relation, but also to the constant adaptation of the product range to consumers' wishes.

Greater flexibility, constant and short-order innovations are what is required. Quality of performance is rapidly gaining in importance. The acceleration of change I touched upon has its mainspring in the interplay between competition and the flexibility of customer wishes.

3. This development is nourished by accelerated technical progress, which in turn profits from the explosion of knowledge which has long been evident. Microelectronics and data processing are examples of this, as is the progress made in biotechnology, and so on.

4. To these changes resulting from the economic dynamic are added political change. Europe may seem to us a political structure, and the transference of national sovereignty to supranational institutions a notable change. Yet the changes taking place in the Eastern Bloc, whose consequences for the Europe of the 1990s and for economic development cannot yet be assessed, are downright dramatic. The decline of socialist systems is very likely to further contribute substantially to the turbulence and symptoms of crisis predicted prior to this development by many forecasters. At the same time, it offers economic opportunities.

5. For the 1990s, it can be predicted with confidence that an even higher degree of significance will be attached to environmental awareness. Surprisingly enough, this manifest development is still frequently repressed or disregarded, one probable reason being that the consequences involved make too high a demand on the imagination. For me it is quite clear, however, that the 'ecological reconstruction of the industrial society' will represent one of the greatest challenges of the 1990s.

There is no need to emphasize that these fields cannot be viewed in isolation, but are interlinked. It is important, therefore, to develop a systemic approach that takes account of this fact.

This list could be extended, but it is sufficient for our consideration. The first inference must be that the challenges of the 1990s cannot be met with traditional answers, and that innovative solutions are required. In this the institutes of higher education must also play a significant role.

Consequences for higher education in Europe

Many of the analyses on which my list of challenges was based are the product of scientists at universities. Yet it is questionable whether these institutes have themselves fully drawn the consequences from them. This would be the more desirable because university education has made an undeniable and indispensable contribution to the history of European economic development. We need only think for example of the figure of the engineer who to this day is fashioned by economically aware faculties and universities. As a further example, let me cite the development of the chemical industry which without university research and graduates and the close connection between higher education and the industry would not have achieved the importance it has today. At the same time, these examples make it clear that it would be mistaken to ascribe the role of the vanguard of economic development to the universities alone. Rather, it appears to be the interplay between certain sectors of the economic system with those of the scientific system which has borne the general development onward.

In any event, it can be said that the quality of the graduates of higher education is of decisive importance for industry and commerce. The transfer of personnel between higher education and industry or commerce is at the same time an important transfer of knowledge, but not the only one. Research and further education, and education of the rising scientific generation, are equally important components.

The question as to whether the European universities are today abreast of the times is one which is not susceptible of a simple answer. Instead, we shall discuss here from the point of view of industry and commerce how the quality of university education in the 1990s must change if a contribution is to be made to the meeting of the challenges which I sketched at the beginning. 'Quality' can be established from the following results and conditions of higher education:

1. Professional and technical knowledge.
2. General knowledge.
3. Formation of attitudes.
4. Length of study.

Let me comment briefly on each of these points.

1.   The main requirement of higher education will continue to be that the graduate must be master of his or her subject. This means that graduates must be able to keep up with scientific developments. A greater significance will, with the advance of broad-based or systemic thinking, accrue to the ability to look beyond the limits of specialist knowledge into other disciplines. This is the old requirement of interdisciplinarity or multidisciplinarity which corresponds to the fact that single-discipline knowledge such as is disseminated in the universities contains only parts of that problem-oriented knowledge which is needed in practice.

The status of indispensable professional, technical knowledge will also increasingly be assigned to the ability to see the European or international dimensions of a subject. I shall discuss later what consequences this may have for the development of European universities.

· The question that divides opinion is the specialization of knowledge. I am one of a large group of practitioners who always prefer the 'generalist' to the 'specialist'. But this view will only be fully understood when I deal with 'Future models of higher education in Europe' (see p. 65).

2.   I myself belong to a generation of university graduates in whose final assessment general knowledge still played a significant part. This was the generation that grew up with the liberal arts (*studium generale*) which, subsequently, for reasons which are common knowledge, were drastically cut back. As far as general knowledge is concerned, it is actually more the schools to which one must turn, but I am convinced that a knowledge of languages and openness

to foreign (European) cultures is a requirement that must also be taken account of by the universities. And this, not only by means of the courses offered. Students must also have the opportunity to acquaint themselves with a foreign language and a foreign country on the spot as a part of their studies. I shall return to this later.

3.   Young people are formed by their time in higher education. At present, German universities at least still tend heavily to the production of 'soloists'. A well-known German industrialist, Ludwig Vaubel, who was especially concerned with the rising generation, once said in this connection that industry needs up to 2 years to make a team member out of a university graduate. Yet efficient teamwork will be decisive for companies that hope to survive in the market in the coming years. The question arises, therefore, as to whether teamwork can be practised during higher education to a greater extent than before, where this is not already happening.

And while we are talking about attitude formation through higher education, we should also mention the 'one-track specialist', the blinkered person who blocks out social changes, sometimes indeed his entire environment, from his perception. Broad-based, systemic thinking is not, of course, primarily a matter of knowledge, but rather one of attitude and approach. It is marked by the desire to perceive things in the context of their interdependence, going beyond the confines of disciplines. I believe that there will be a constantly increasing demand in industry and commerce for people who possess a social and environmental sensitivity enabling companies to react more easily to future and present demands in these fields.

Finally, it must be emphasized that nobody ever completes their education at university. Higher education is only a stage in the process of a lifetime of learning. The function of higher education should therefore also include practice of and preparation for this life-long learning process.

4.   The quality of higher education is also dependent on length of study. Here the differences between the various European countries are very marked. In the Federal Republic of Germany, an average of 14 semesters is currently the norm. Higher education specialists may well object that the numerous requirements listed above would lead rather to a prolongation of courses of studies than to their shortening. However, it must be stated that courses extending beyond 5 years are generally agreed by industry and commerce to be too long. The reasons for this are a belated entry into the world of work and, thus, a diminished prospect of graduates adapting to this new environment.

The quality profile of higher education that I have sketched here – professional and technical knowledge, general knowledge, attitude formation and length of study – can naturally only provide some points of departure. My information is doubtless incomplete when I assume that at present there is scarcely any European higher education system which fully meets all these requirements. Nor are they likely to be met if new models of higher education are not developed or tried out.

Future models of higher education in Europe

It can hardly be expected of this chapter that it should deal more comprehensively with a new conception of higher education. Elements of such a conception can already be found here and there; some of them indeed have been around for some time. We must also look to old ideals of higher education when addressing the future.

First, I should like to return to the consequences of the explosion of knowledge I mentioned earlier. In conjunction with the acceleration of change, it has led to the life-long learning process and thus higher education at universities gaining increasing importance. In this connection, I am going to propound the possibly provocative-sounding thesis that, despite the realization of the necessity for life-long learning, the consequences are not, or are only in embryonic form, to be noted in the education system. As a rule, most schools still do not educate for continued learning, or do so only imperfectly. This may apply less to those who will become students than to those who on leaving school and vocational training will have 'completed' their education. But life-long learning also has a decisive consequence for higher education: in the place of a practically self-contained higher education comprising the specializations it would be possible to envisage a shorter, more compact basic education to which specializations must be, not immediately thereafter, built-on. It would be perfectly feasible to provide for specializations and supplementations to be subsequently built-on concurrently with, or in alternation with, the exercise of the profession. This could involve a combination of open university and university attendance. Such a sequence of higher education, involving study units and further education, could mean that the time that has to be spent in higher education prior to the first professional activity is shortened. At the same time, the course of study would be stimulated through the input of practical experience by the students

Such models not only make considerable demands in the field of organization of higher education. They can only be implemented if industry and commerce can come up with a solution to the problem of study-release.

The advantages of practical experience are also proved by models of combined study and work. In this connection, the German polytechnics (*Fachhochschulen*) especially have gained experience. I myself can quote the recent example of a 2-year motor vehicle construction course in which the Fachhochschule Braunschweig-Wolfenbüttel cooperates with vehicle manufacturers, chiefly Volkswagen AG.

As an initial conclusion of the discussion so far, it can thus be stated that all models of higher education which seek to reinforce the practical element require the cooperation of industry and commerce. As far as I can judge, the willingness to cooperate has significantly increased. The confederations of industry and commerce also encourage their member companies in this respect. I believe that a stronger emphasis on practical work will be of benefit not only to the students direct but also to the courses, and will help to bridge the gap between the economic system and the scientific system.

We now come to a second element, which in my view must be an indispensable component of a new conception of higher education. When I enrolled at the University of Hamburg, I was told regretfully – since pious wishes were the currency of the overcrowded universities of Germany in the immediate post-war period – that I would have to change universities once, and also include semesters abroad in my planning. The reasons given for this were avoidance of a one-sided education and an acquaintance with the internationality of science. This recommendation is in no way superannuated. I believe that future models of higher education should profit from the experience already gained in respect of study periods abroad. It should be possible to complete part of the course in one's home country and another part abroad. Various combinations are possible here, which from the viewpoint of industry and commerce – in so far as these are internationally oriented or European in nature – are gaining great importance. I know about the problems and obstacles involved in matching courses and diplomas or degrees one to another; but there are already a number of partnerships between universities in various European countries promoting student exchange. This represents a very important task which can bear much fruit, not only in the technical, but also in the human sphere. The reactions from German industry and commerce which have reached me are, without exception, positive.

The mission of the European universities

A discussion of the quality of higher education from the viewpoint of industry and commerce must anticipate a misunderstanding which could arise from my comments. Even if the universities are essential agents of economic development, and through higher education are indispensable for the efficiency of industry and commerce, the impression must not be given that the institutions of higher education should be made the servant of business.

In my view, the social function of a university is defined by two concepts: receptiveness and detachment. Let me explain this. Society, and thus industry and commerce, expect the universities to be receptive to their problems. This does not necessarily mean offering a solution to them, but at least an open ear, accessibility, a readiness to engage in dialogue. I know – never has an academic institution turned a completely deaf ear to such a dialogue. We need think only of individual contacts, meetings in the practical sphere, and so on. The receptiveness I refer to is evidenced by the active interest shown by a university in its environment – the preparedness to address problems, by which is meant fundamentally the entire breadth of the 'problem landscape' outside of the university. Naturally, however, the demand for receptiveness and practical orientation can give rise to mistrust and fears, e.g. that fundamental research could be neglected or that a too-decisive shift in the direction of socio-economic utilitarianism may occur.

It is for this reason that I emphasized the second concept: detachment. Detachment can be defined as the requisite degree of aloofness of science from everyday problems, the more fundamental apprehension of problems, the preoccupation with questions of generality. Scientific knowledge is achieved in many areas only when distanced from practical problems. But one should not make the mistake of confusing this detachment with the ivory tower: that is not detachment, but isolation.

From the viewpoint of the economic practicality in which I function, but also on the basis of many years' university teaching, I would stress that both are necessary if the university is to fulfil its tasks, which include that of education: receptiveness *and* detachment. Standing aside from practicality is an advantage, so long as it is not stand-offishness (which basically only betrays a fear of contact) but an habitual standing back for the purpose of arriving at balanced, unaffected, more objective judgements. Detachment without receptiveness turns into isolation, receptiveness without detachment into a failure to carry out the scientific task. Higher education is an economic necessity, a means of promoting innovation, and we can only hope that the development of modern European companies into 'learning companies' (Meyer-Dohm, 1988) will be accompanied by an improvement in the quality of higher education. The fact that efforts are already being made at some universities, and results have been achieved, is an encouraging sign.

Bibliography

Albach, H., Busse von Colbe, W. and Sabel, H. (eds) (1978). *Lebenslanges Lernen*. Wiesbaden: Gabler.

Duddeck, H. (1988). Ingenieure für die Zukunft. In Bachmann, S., Bohnet, M. and Lompe, K. (eds), *Industriegesellschaft im Wandel*, pp. 147–67. Hildesheim: Olms.

Grochla, E. (1978). Lernprozesse im Rahmen der Organisationsplanung und entwick-lung. In Albach, H., Busse von Colbe, W. and Sabel, H. (eds), *Lebenslanges Lernen*, pp. 51–99. Wiesbaden: Gabler.

Lamszus, H. and Sanmann, H. (eds) (1987). *Neue Technologien, Arbeitsmarkt und Berufs-qualifikation*. Stuttgart: Haupt.

Meyer-Dohm, P. (1988). Bildungsarbeit im lernenden Unternehmen. In Meyer-Dohm, P., Tuchtfeldt, E. and Wesner, E. (eds), *Der Mensch im Unternehmen*, pp. 249–71. Stuttgart: Haupt.

Meyer-Dohm, P. and Schütze, H. G. (eds) (1987). *Technischer Wandel und Qualifizierung: Die neue Synthese*. Frankfurt: Campus.

7

Personal Transferable Skills for Employment: The Role of Higher Education

Ann Bailey

Within their academic courses, some higher education establishments already foster the behavioural or transferable life skills that are essential to the future of industry both in this, and the next, decade. Others have yet to recognize the need for their students to be taught anything besides purely academic/research subjects. Industry needs well-rounded individuals. People who know their own strengths and weaknesses and how to maximize the one and minimize the other; who understand and appreciate the necessity of accepting responsibility for their own lives, their career progression, and their development. Everyone must realize that learning is a lifetime process that does not stop on leaving higher education. Higher education must ensure that students understand this.

It is important for industry to have an adaptable and flexible workforce, one that is capable of acquiring whatever skills may be relevant to the changing times and environment. That, needless to say, is largely a matter of attitude. Individuals must be able to handle the process of change: to understand change and their reaction to it and to work positively with change rather than to oppose it. It has been estimated that most people will make at least four major shifts in their working lives – and that does not necessarily mean changing employers. In high-tech companies, the figure will rise to about eight major changes; within my own company eight is a conservative figure! This will mean that people will have to train and retrain as the need arises.

Between us, we in industry and those in higher education need to engender a more positive attitude to the modern high-tech environment, to recognize the importance of industry to the economy of the country and society, and also to increase awareness of the opportunities that it offers. Technology has a major role to play and students must be prepared to work with it, with information technology in particular. It is not important to know exactly how technology works, but it is vital to understand how it can work for us: how to use it as a tool to 'get the job done'. We must work to break down the stereotypes and role models that currently exist in students' attitudes to technology. Higher education students, and particularly female students, must realize that they should not restrict their options but, in fact, should actively seek to take additional courses to enhance their career opportunities. Higher education must endeavour to integrate technology into all its disciplines as a matter of course. Industry must also ensure that it offers challenging opportunities to graduates, no matter what their gender or discipline.

One area where there is a major difference between the ways in which education and industry operate is that of teamwork. In general, our education system is based on individual work and collaboration is frowned upon. Our HE examination system is one in which students often have to learn facts and regurgitate them – the students who can remember most are given the highest awards. Understanding and being able to apply what is learned to a real-life problem is often neither examined nor rewarded. The ability of students to work with colleagues to 'deliver the goods' by a set date is given little prominence, despite being a key element in the world of work. Teamwork demands a great deal of the individual: it is not just a question of being able to 'get on' with others; it is about the ability to communicate well, both verbally and in writing; and of being able to understand non-verbal messages given by colleagues and thus of being sensitive to the feelings and needs of others. It concerns trust and the ability to share ideas – to gain kudos for the group rather than for the individual.

What, then, can higher education do to foster these qualities in its students? It would help greatly if staff development activities were organized to enable tutors to recognize how they could integrate the development of practical transferable life/personal skills training into their courses. Obviously, where tutors do not possess these skills, it would be necessary to provide a training programme for them. This, undoubtedly, would cost both money and time, but it is an example of a situation in which industry and education could collaborate effectively. Another way forward would be for companies to sponsor tutors on external courses or even to make free places available to tutors in their in-house training programmes, or even, perhaps, to send a trainer to run a workshop in a higher education institution. To make this possible education would, of course, need to support its staff by providing teaching cover for those undergoing training.

In many institutions, personal skills development already exists, especially in business studies and related courses. Higher education often possesses expertise itself which could be utilized to develop its members of staff, but frequently it fails to recognize, or perhaps make effective use of, this potential.

Soon, many students coming to HE will have already been exposed to forms of learning that emphasize practice and will, in consequence, expect these skills and abilities to be present in their higher educational courses. I have heard students say that because someone had told them something it did not mean that they could do it. They would need to be able to try things for themselves: to show what they could, or could not, do.

Students must be aware of their levels of skill, what is needed to raise them, and how this can be achieved during the development of their professional competencies. Unfortunately, even when they are exposed to personal skills development, they all-too-often do not realize exactly what they have learned.

They do not, for example, think to include references to these skills in their curricula vitae. More needs to be done to help them to appreciate what, apart from the obvious academic knowledge, they have learned in the course of their studies, and to assist them to use the transferable skills and competencies that they have gained when applying for employment at the end of their courses.

One of the difficulties in developing skill and competency is assessment. I believe that this is mainly an attitudinal problem, as I have heard it said that students will not accept the assessment of skill, but I believe that they will if the right expectations are set initially: if the right support, controls, evaluation and monitoring are put into place; if there is a positive attitude from the academic staff; and if employers not only recognize, but also voice, the importance of it. Much has to be done to change the attitudes of both HE and employers. That is no reason, however, why we should not embark on the task. We cannot succeed unless we start. Again, I believe that the expertise of both partners – industry and education – could be used in joint work to produce an acceptable solution. I appreciate that there is still the problem of the validation of degrees and that, in the main, only academic knowledge is deemed measurable. If we start first by getting the different skills and measurements integrated into courses and prove that this 'works', we can then provide a much better base from which to lobby for changes in validation.

HE can also help students to appreciate the fact that some employers already assess life and personal skills during interviews. They can do this by providing the student with information on the various types of interviews that they use, and by explaining the necessity of marketing the skills they have been developing. Employers can assist by running seminars or workshops on this subject for higher educational establishments.

Employers who have already realized the need to assess these different areas have developed a variety of ways of collecting data. Most commonly they do it through the initial sifting of curricula vitae or application forms, to enable students who are aware of the value of these skills to come to the fore. By being able to demonstrate their command of self-knowledge and learning, they tend to be selected for interview. Even where there is an established set of criteria against which to sift applicants, selection of candidates for interview is often carried out as a 'gut-feel' reaction to the quality of the application. If the students have recognized the necessity of a curriculum vitae as a means to 'sell' themselves, and have learned how to produce one, they will score strongly on measures of capability.

When being interviewed, applicants will have to demonstrate that these life/personal skills are not just 'head knowledge' but an integral part of themselves. Those employers whose interviews are behaviourally based, usually establish a set of the behavioural skills (and definitions of those skills) which are needed for the job that the applicant is being interviewed for. They will expect students to be able to give examples of work in these areas: what they have done, what they learned from doing it, how they would have changed things if given the opportunity to repeat the process, and why. In other words, they will be asked what they would do in a given situation, why they would do it, what would be the results, how they would do it differently the next time, and why. Such interviews tend to be lengthy, and employers who use them will therefore be committed to spending considerable time with applicants to try to understand them. Employers need concrete data on which to make decisions: for example, they will try to infer from a given situation, whether the applicant demonstrated problem analysis skill; what he or she did and said; and what were the results.

Another method of collecting data for selection purposes is to set up group-based activities. Here all the applicants are brought together, sometimes in a management assessment/development centre, for group assessment exercises. Again, this type of activity requires a great deal of organizing, resourcing and monitoring. Employers, therefore, wish to see only those candidates who can respond well in these circumstances. These activities sort out those who have been given training, even if it has only been very basic. The development of these skills will allow students to give a better account of themselves.

Recently, there has been a great deal of talk about student 'profiling'. This – if established in the right manner with a common format – could provide an excellent insight into the student for a potential employer. However, students must feel that they own the profile, which should contain self-assessment and inputs from various sources – tutors, peers, vacation employers – and must show the progress and development of the individual. Until documents of this sort have been tried and tested by students, tutors and employers, their validity cannot be established and their usefulness understood. This again is a field where industry could work with education to develop methods acceptable to both parties, which would allow students to demonstrate all their competencies, not simply their academic achievements.

HE offers many examples of good practice in the development of personal transferable skills. For example, at Bradford University some students in the second year of their courses have to research, develop and present a case on a subject of public concern. They work in groups making contact with contractors, residents, environmentalists, the local council and whoever else is appropriate. They prepare their case and present it. This educational experience aids the development of teamwork, communication skills, problem analysis and judgement. These qualities are self-consciously reviewed and discussed during the monitoring and evaluation process. This project has encouraged Bradford University to establish strong external links. One of the keys to enable HE to develop the necessary skills in students, is the establishment of a variety of partnerships, particularly with industry.

The high-tech world is a fast-moving, ever-changing environment which, as I have said, needs people who have the capacity to learn and develop, to move and change with the needs of the organization: who are prepared to break the mould of the past. Education, and in particular higher education, is an important supplier of future managers and leaders of industry. For these reasons, I believe it is not only important, but also vital, that links between HE and industry are developed. Companies need to incorporate links in their strategic and business plans. HE must be prepared to change teaching methods to include elements of personal/life skills tuition for their students.

When developing their strategic plans, companies need to consider their reasons for proposing to allocate time, resources, money and effort into forming and developing links with HE. Understanding this will help them to determine where the major support should be targeted. Once the mission, or *raison d'être*, has been established and commitment made, the size of the budget has to be decided, together with the time-scale and methods for monitoring and evaluating the effectiveness of the project. It is important that commitment, at a senior level, is sustained and not simply a flash in the pan – which would cause frustration and could make the programme ineffective. Smaller companies should recognize that their contributions of time, money, personnel and materials must reflect their relative size and cannot equal those of large companies.

HE must realize that it already has a range of abilities in the enterprise area that can be developed further. A different approach to teaching and learning styles, to include life-skills training for all students, will, no doubt, be difficult for some members of staff to come to terms with. Such a change will require both commitment and training to be successfully achieved. It will be hard for some staff, and students, to accept that lectures alone do not develop the life-skills that students need to possess. It will also be difficult to recognize that, since the traditional style rarely generates enthusiasm or motivates students, staff themselves must learn new skills. In consequence, the motivated and keen members of staff, who are prepared to develop themselves and work in new ways, will need to be rewarded significantly.

In working with HE establishments that are encouraging enterprise activities – with or without government money – I have found that when the three partners (students, tutors and industrialists) get together, much can be achieved. If progress is to be made, such a partnership needs to encourage teamwork, to ensure effective communication (including active listening), to manage change, to be sensitive to the needs of others in the group, to lead to creative thinking, and to demonstrate both problem-solving and decision-making abilities.

Industry cannot expect HE to do all the work itself – there must be a partnership as both sides have the potential to gain from a closer relationship. Employers cannot assume that HE will teach personal skills programmes that will satisfy their needs if they do not contribute to the development of standards that are acceptable to all the partners. There must be a shared body of knowledge that is intergrated into educational courses, and on which industry and the students' life experiences can build.

Let us remember the old adage, 'united we stand, divided we fall' – so it is with the industry and education partnership. Separately we may flounder and struggle; together we have the potential to achieve so much – a strong base from which tomorrow's employees will be able to grow and develop. That will help to build a successful future for us all.

Part 4

Changes in Culture and Organization

8

The Shifting Culture of Higher Education

John Fielden

This chapter focuses on the internal structures of higher education institutions and the changes that have been taking place within them. These are analysed to identify any clear trends or basic changes in culture. Finally, the current managerial cultures in business are compared and the question 'Has higher education got the balance of culture right?' is considered.

Trends in culture

'The new director of the course must be an academic leader, must possess entrepreneurial ability and the capacity to inspire confidence both within the University and outside.' So ran a report in 1989 to the General Board of the University of Cambridge on a proposal to develop an MBA course. The inclusion of the concept of entrepreneurialism would have been unthinkable 10 years before and neatly sums up the changes that have occurred in culture. The Training Agency's Enterprise in Higher Education (EHE) initiative evoked a remarkable response from a community that might have been thought suspicious of commercial implants in the curriculum. Nearly all non-university HE institutions and three-quarters of universities submitted bids for EHE funding. An external academic evaluation reported that 'there is a very wide feeling that not to bid shows hostility to the enterprise culture' (Williams, 1989). It could be argued that this response is a Pavlovian reaction to the availability of funds and shows little more than a flexible, or even cynical, willingness to seek income. Taken together with other reactions and initiatives in higher education institutions, however, the response does ring true. Consider the following examples of actions or initiatives in 1989:

- When asked to state their overall objectives, a majority of universities gave a primary aim as being to increase their income from non-University Funding Council (UFC) sources.
- The UFC and Polytechnics and Colleges Funding Council (PCFC) had

small pump-priming funds for fund-raising initiatives. Both were heavily oversubscribed and institutions subsequently jostled to appoint appeal or development fund directors.

- Senior management training programmes for PCFC institutions contained prominent courses on marketing and customer culture.
- New criteria crept into appointments processes for heads of schools or deans; management skills, financial competence or entrepreneurial awareness were openly stated as factors. Within universities, some vice-chancellors succeeded in appointing key academics to management positions, rather than inheriting deans who were democratically elected.

There were financial consequences to the creeping managerialism. In the PCFC sector, some directors seized on their chief executive functions eagerly and sought matching financial rewards. Under the terms of the 1988 Education Reform Act, their remuneration and that of the 'senior staff' came outside national pay bargaining and within the remit of the corporation's governing body. Settlements of £50 000 to £60 000, plus car, were reported for some polytechnic directors, allied to short-term contracts and the appraisal of performance. The risk-taking academic manager with low job security became a real model. Whether governing bodies will ever invoke the performance criteria and terminate a contract has yet to be seen.

Generalizations about higher educational institutions are never easy or realistic. The extremes of history, size and culture within even the UFC umbrella produce a range from Salford to Cambridge, St David's Lampeter to the London School of Economics. The spectrum widens further with the PCFC institutions embracing a conglomerate like the London Institute, a host of small monotechnics and large broadly based polytechnics like the Polytechnic of Central London or Manchester. The arrival of independence for PCFC institutions in April 1989 has certainly spurred many to go further in cultural and managerial terms than the Act strictly required. It was just possible to slide easily into independence with help from a cooperative local education authority without introducing many innovations in managerial style or culture and a few chose this course, preferring to minimize upheaval. At the other extreme, however, the more managerially orientated institution is likely to have:

- Redefined the roles and titles of its senior academic post holders, and placed them on performance-related contracts.
- Introduced strategic planning, independently of the PCFC-inspired timetable, and linked institutional and departmental (or school) objectives.
- Considered its markets and clientele, and as a result planned the introduction of new courses which meet the needs it has identified.
- Seen the quality of physical resources in general, and student accommodation in particular, as linked to marketing success.
- Targeted non-PCFC income sources such as PICKUP, the European Community programmes and EHE and set out a policy for collaboration with business.

The striking conclusion from most observers of higher education in 1989 is that so many institutions have adopted all the above strategies and so many others are aspiring to them. A significant adoption of managerial cultures is taking place at senior levels. At the 'chalk face', however, anxiety about the entrepreneurial tendencies is still evident. In order to see how institutions are facing these pressures, we shall look at organizational forms and trends.

Trends in organization and structure

The Jarratt Report and the advent of incorporation provided the spurs for UFC and PCFC institutions, respectively, to consider their organization and structure. As already mentioned, generalizations can be misleading, but some changes may be highlighted:

1. The growing willingness of vice-chancellors or directors to adopt the role (suitably modified) of chief executive. The phrase found its way into several sets of 'further particulars' for new appointments. It was adopted more openly by some heads of PCFC institutions and the Committee of Polytechnic Directors used it as the generic term for heads.
2. The acceptance within UFC institutions of the need for full-time senior executive management. Leicester University's unique designation of an executive pro-vice-chancellor and registrar and Imperial College's appointment of a senior industrialist as managing director were part of the same trend.
3. The designation within a significant number of PCFC institutions of a directorate level post with responsibility for marketing and income generation.
4. The almost universal adoption of the directorate or 'management team' concept of a small group of senior officers enjoying delegated authority from the council or governing body to take key decisions.
5. The disillusion of federal universities with their complex, hierarchical structures led to a series of reports or reviews, not all consistent in their findings (Wass on Cambridge, Smith on London and Daniel on Wales).

The internal structures of higher educational institutions were almost all under review and subject to change. The following general themes were found in most cases:

1. The need to absorb new management positions devoted to functions such as corporate planning, information technology (IT) strategy, staff training, or staff appraisal (marketing has already been referred to).
2. A grouping of academic departments within 'schools', faculties or 'areas' in order to encourage cohesive interdisciplinary developments with the side benefit of reducing the number of senior academic managers needed.
3. The development of devolved planning and budgeting processes intended to provide incentives to the new breed of academic manager.

4. Consequential tension over the balance of roles and powers between the newly enfranchised budget managers and the centre with its aggressive corporate ambitions and plans.

As the 1990s began, there were more questions than answers to the problems of structure and organization. In general, decentralization of decision making was the dominant theme, but the new directorates saw a key role for themselves in steering the course of their institution. Who should have what power at what level was a difficult issue and solutions tended to be based on individuals and their respective personalities rather than on management theory. As performance-related pay becomes a standard at senior levels in higher education, it will be essential for the issues of accountability and responsibility to be fully worked out. If they are not, individuals will be paid for 'performance' to which they have contributed nothing, or will make impressive plans which achieve nothing because of the absence of sufficient management authority.

Thus, higher educational institutions (HEIs) have embarked on significant experimentation in organizational and structural terms. They have not been alone in the public sector as similar changes have rippled through the Civil Service (cf. Financial Management Initiative and Next Steps), the Health Service (Griffiths Report and the 1989 White Papers) and almost all recipients of public money. It has been assumed that all these changes have been based on best private practice and that by adopting them the public sector was simply 'catching up'. We shall now examine this claim in the context of higher education and see whether there is an easy, relevant transfer of principles and practice from the private to the public sectors.

Business practice

During the 1980s, private sector organizations in the UK have faced up to numerous new management challenges. Their responses have involved many of the same mechanisms or techniques as have been described above for HEIs. The principal examples are:

1. A move away from large conglomerate structures to smaller business units in which managers are held accountable for business performance.
2. Primacy of the marketing function over the production function; customers are the predominant influence on company fortunes and new manufacturing and IT techniques make it possible to produce immediately in response to market needs, eliminating stockholding.
3. A greater emphasis on people, investment in training and a long-term view of skills and peoples' capability, thus beginning a reversal of the attitude that people could be acquired or disposed of as the market dictated.
4. A search for the right balance between central control and devolution of management responsibility.
5. Acceptance that company success is not simply measured by bottom line or

profit, but that longer-term criteria require investment in social, charitable, environmental or education projects. Closer links with higher education have acquired strategic importance rather than mere public relations value: 'From the Company's point of view a productive relationship with higher education can make a major contribution to its competitiveness and business performance' (DTI, 1989).

6. Greater weight given internally in companies to the human resource or personnel function so that appraisal, performance-related pay and other processes can operate effectively.
7. Quality of the product or service is seen as important a factor as price. The responsibility for achieving quality is widely spread throughout an organization rather than being a check after the production process.

Management thinking in the 1980s largely followed the tenets of Peters and Waterman's 'In Search of Excellence' (despite the low success rate of many of the corporations praised in the text) and UK management works focused on the same concept: delegation, niche marketing, human resource strategies, IT for competitive advantage, global corporate strategies, etc.

The common features with developments in HEIs will have become clear. What is not so obvious is the reason for the success or failure of some transfers. What are the special features of management in HEIs which must overlay any private sector techniques? The answers are partly in the nature of HEIs themselves and partly in the culture which they must have to prosper. Among the principal factors of HEIs are:

1. Academic organizations are not authoritarian; individuals within them are self-motivated, driven either by dedication to teaching or research, or personal academic ambitions to build up departments or institutions. Thus, people can be encouraged and given incentives to perform, but not easily instructed.
2. The community values individual freedoms to choose research careers or programmes, irrespective of short-term political or commercial pressure. Thus, while the power of the purse will always be influential in directing research activities, the essence of an HEI is that some enquiry will be self-funded and unplanned.
3. HEIs, although composed of disparate and competing disciplines, are quick to unite against a common threat and their 'middle managers' want to feel consulted in key institutional decisions. Thus, most strategic planning cycles must be a careful blend of bottom-up and top-down processes.
4. Budgetary devolution to heads should not have profit or income generation as the sole arbiters of success, since some disciplines will have little potential for excelling in these areas. Thus, there will always need to be central 'corporate' sponsorship for some of the institutions' services.
5. Performance is very hard to quantify and performance indicators are not readily available. The purely quantitative indicators can be highly misleading if taken on their own, as the quality of teaching and research output are vital elements in the institution's performance.

The management of a higher education institution is not only very different from the management of a commercial enterprise, but also much more difficult. The interrelationship of qualitative and quantitative factors in most decisions present continual value judgements to decision makers. The most efficient or economical decision is not always the soundest; information systems must record and rank qualitative and quantitative data; management hierarchies must be able to listen to specialist evidence from external sources since there are no internal peers for some courses or services.

It is clear that, despite the obvious differences and difficulties, many recent transfers of private sector management cultures into HEIs are both relevant and beneficial. We shall conclude by examining this further and ask whether the correct balance is being achieved.

The balance of culture

There are two extremes of opinion on the advent of management cultures into HEIs. The one, variously labelled as hawkish, Thatcherite and incorrectly affiliated with the Jarratt Report, suggests that institutions are long overdue for a full injection of private sector management techniques. There is nothing special about them, it is argued, and a thorough application of cost-control and efficiency techniques would be immediately productive. The converse view has recently been presented by Dame Mary Warnock. If we tamper too much with the structures and processes of HEIs, we will damage their essential creativity and freedoms.

Most institutional managers will place themselves between these two extremes of opinion. They will regard the introduction of some management principles as essential, but will also respect the strongly held academic view that in some cases there are qualitative grounds for overruling the verdict of an efficiency or 'value-for-money' exercise. An institution must preserve its academic shape and research programmes in areas which are not immediately economic or productive. Industry also sympathizes with this approach; it is not as dedicated to profit and short-term horizons as critics of higher education sometimes suggest.

> Companies have unanimously told the Council for Industry and Higher Education that they greatly value pure and curiosity-led research as the seed-bed from which their own applied work can develop marketable technologies. They wish to see neither a reduction in the overall science base nor any significant shift by the universities towards applied work which is easier to 'sell' (CIHE, 1987).

Deciding where to place an institution's management style between the two extremes is a key task for its chief executive. He or she has to set the tone for management change to suit the institution. Cranfield and Cambridge have vastly differing cultures and management processes, yet each produces highly regarded postgraduates for different markets by different methods. The

Cranfield culture has, however, been developed and grown over a 10-year period – admittedly from a unique foundation – by its former vice-chancellor. It represents possibly the most extreme example of the injection of commercial values and processes into a higher educational institution. These values and processes are not necessarily partners and this is the key distinction. There is no possible disadvantage from importing the best private sector processes and techniques into HEI management. These systems and mechanics should merely be the framework for value judgements, and as long as the key values remain, the essential nature of the academic institution will survive. Here again, we return to a key role of the chief executive in setting and maintaining the correct values in the institution's management and decision-making processes.

References

CIHE (1987). *Towards a Partnership*. London: Council for Industry and Higher Education.

DTI (1989). *Policy and Strategy for Companies, Collaboration between Business and Higher Education*. Department of Trade and Industry/Council for Industry and Higher Education. London: HMSO.

Williams, G. (1989). *Monitoring and Evaluation of New Funding Mechanisms in Higher Education*. Information Bulletin No. 4. London: Institute of Education.

9

A Responsive Higher Education System

Anne Jones

Our higher education system, with its roots in the best of medieval tradition, has classically been immune from the slings and arrows of outrageous economic fortune: the purposes of higher education are primarily the pursuit of knowledge, truth and beauty for its own sake. Total immersion in an atmosphere of calm, reflection and learning is critical for the development of pure thought, and students must *not* be subject to the pressures of the economy, the demands of working life, or the pressures of having to manage their own everyday lives. It is very difficult to combine the pursuit of knowledge with the practicalities of life. There is a strong argument for ivory towers.

Yet, this is not the scene we now find ourselves in, for both good and bad reasons. Higher educational institutions have never before felt so acutely the meaning of 'the economic imperative'. Attracting lucrative research projects, sponsorship from employers for facilities and people, crumbs of funding from this government agency or that international fund, pennies from heaven via the donations of erstwhile scholars, this kind of Bosch-like landscape, a nightmare become reality, draws senior college administrators into new and terrifying territories. What is higher education about now? The 'enterprise' culture is certainly biting hard at the foundations of higher educational life, but what is it doing to the students? They too are in a harsher financial regime, with the prospect of loans, with less residential provision, and a tendency for students to self-cater because it is cheaper. But what about their education? The way students now learn will vary enormously from place to place, and subject to subject. It is still possible for students to learn in the way that I did some 40 years ago: in a calm and relaxed atmosphere with only a few lectures a week and hardly any written work (though that scenario always applied more to arts than to science undergraduates). But what is coming now, more and more, is a change in the way students learn, and want to learn, and the ways in which this connects with life after HE – that is to say, with the world of work.

In my day, the emphasis was on a degree for its own sake: no matter whether it was 'useful' in one's future job. In fact, it was considered rather *infra dig.* even to *think* about any connection with work. My own choice of modern languages because it was 'more useful' than other arts degrees, turned out to be misplaced – it really was only fully useful in teaching!

But now, students themselves come with a different set of expectations and experiences, employers are more articulate about what they want from graduates, and government is beginning to intervene in the processes. The very idea of a 'work-related higher education curriculum', while it might cause some academic staff to turn red (or white), is now on the agenda. As E. M. Forster put it, 'only connect!': making the connections between academic learning and vocational usefulness is now very much a concern of higher education as well as schools and colleges.

This fundamental change in the culture of education has been greatly influenced by the Royal Society of Arts' (RSA) Education for Capability movement. In 1983, a group of people at the RSA signed a manifesto supporting the idea of getting education to be as much concerned about capability as about knowledge. By capability was meant the application of knowledge, the ability to do and complete a task, to solve problems, to use initiative, be enterprising, be self-managing, creative and practical. The signatories of this manifesto included a large number of leading thinkers and academics. The effect of the Education for Capability movement has been to influence government policy and educational practice at all levels.

The RSA itself held an annual award ceremony, which gained great recognition and gave status to this important movement. Initial emphasis was on secondary education, but current interest and activity lies in both further and higher education.

Government policy has taken up the same theme. In 1983, the government launched the Technical and Vocational Education Initiative (TVEI), which sought to make education 14–18 more relevant to the needs of employers. In 1987, the TVEI was made a *national* initiative, a 10-year programme designed to change the culture of the whole secondary educational system and to affect the education of all students aged 14–18. TVEI is a strategy for the management of change, which has not only made new demands on teachers and pupils, but which has also supported them in this. It now covers the whole curriculum (and very much supports the national curriculum) and all local education authorities (LEAs). It seeks to equip young people for the demands of working life on a rapidly changing world economy by the following means:

1. To relate what is learned in school to the world of work.
2. To make sure that all young people are scientifically and technologically literate (including information technology skills) and able to speak more than one other language.
3. To ensure that young people have experience of work and do projects in 'real settings' so that they understand the world of work better.
4. To help teaching and learning styles to change so that young people learn *how*, as well as what, can manage their own learning, can work with and through other people, can use modern technology as a tool of learning.
5. To improve the system of guidance counselling and progression, to help

young people set goals and targets for their learning, to provide a record of achievement which records *capability* as well as academic achievement, and to help young people see 16+ as a stepping stone to further learning, not the end of it all.

TVEI is gradually working its way through the system. In the pilot phase, it mainly attracted young people who wanted to leave school at 16, but now that it is catering for the whole ability range, a *lot* of TVEI graduates will be going on to higher education. The first 18-year-olds coming out of the first 11 LEAs in TVEI extension will be applying for places in higher education in October 1992. If all goes according to plan, I can confidently predict that these TVEI graduates will be articulate, capable, enterprising, information technology (IT) literate, well motivated, good at working individually and in teams, aware of employers' needs and the nature of working life, and confident. Not all to the same degree, of course; but a great deal more so than previous generations. And by 1994, the vast majority of the nation's 18-year-old school-leavers will have been through this process. By 1996, all 18-year-old school-leavers will also have been through the National Curriculum with its broad and balanced subject spread and its very demanding attainment targets, economic and industrial awareness, and so on.

It is important to remember at this stage that there will be *fewer* 18-year-olds around in the mid-1990s – nearly a third less than now. The hope is that more of them will go on to higher education: thus the current 14–15% participation rate will rise to 18–20%, keeping the numbers at par, or slightly on the increase. Many people hope that the participation rate will go up even more for there is over demand from employers for graduates.

However, the undergraduates of the early 1990s, who are in fact TVEI National Curriculum graduates, will have different expectations of the system, and different experiences to bring to bear on that system.

They will want and expect more active learning styles, they will want to use computers, they may be used to 'flexible learning' (i.e. open or distanced learning, supported self-study, interactive video; they will certainly be used to designing and doing projects in teams, making presentations, negotiating with the outside world, and so on). So they will start off from an increasingly different base – they will be less passive, and there will be less 'waiting to be told what to do next'! The best students have, of course, always been like this, and some will never be like this however 'TVEI'd' they have been. Many HE institutions themselves already expect and encourage this kind of approach to learning. But those which do not, may find that their traditional teaching methods are challenged. This in itself could be an exciting stimulus to growth and development – again the best students have always challenged the system and helped it to remain in touch with the outside world.

A further feature of the student population of the mid-1990s will be its ethnicity, its gender, and its age. There is already evidence that the best academic students in Britain today are not the indigenous whites but the Indians, closely followed by the Chinese. Further, the gender gap at 18 is rapidly closing and there are at last more UCCA applications made by females than males. And, finally, many more 'older' people, those who for various reasons did not go on to higher education when they were 18, are now managing to catch up in later life. These more mature students will not want to be spoon-fed either – they will have held down responsible jobs, mortgages and had families and they will have as much to contribute to the HE system as to take from it.

Many of these older people coming into HE will have come to this point via further education, which itself has a key role to play in getting older people 'access' to higher education. When older students do not have appropriate 'A' levels (or any 'A' levels), when they have lost the habit of studying, they need some kind of transition first to make sure their qualifications are appropriate and relevant, and also to make sure they know how to learn. Part of this process is to assess what they know and can do already: they may not have 'A' levels, but they might have been holding down a job of considerable technical complexity and responsibility. Their existing competence and capabilities need to be properly assessed and accredited, what we call now 'the assessment of prior learning'. It will be inappropriate for all students to take all parts of all HE courses when they already know, understand and can do what the theory is about. So credit transfers and modular accreditation come into play here.

Not all older people will want to be full-time students – it may be inappropriate, unnecessary or inconvenient for them to give up their full-time jobs, so as to learn full-time. Many of these students can, and will, be helped by further education colleges, by higher education and by their employers working in partnership to get higher level qualifications by a part-time flexible modular route. Whether or not higher education likes this idea, the fact is that the demand will be there, and those educational institutions that can meet these demands will find themselves very much in business. And in some cases Mohammed will have to go to the mountain: that is to say that not all higher education will take place in the college; much of it will take place at work, either because the lecturer goes there, or because of open learning methods which make it possible, for example, for workers to have a lecture delivered from the other side of the world. The market for higher education will be *international*: it may not be necessary for overseas students normally to travel from their own countries, or at least, not for the whole 3 years. The Open University, Open Polytechnic and Open College movements are all precursors of this trend. But as the globe shrinks and intercontinental communication becomes an everyday occurrence, we need to remember to think both globally and locally simultaneously.

In thinking locally, higher education institutions will want to make sure they are in touch with local employers and in particular with the Training and Enterprise Councils which are government-funded, employer-led bodies with the remit and the resources to commission both further and higher education institutions to upskill and update the local workforce: hence the need for more flexible forms of delivery, non-residential, part-time and off-site. Many local people who are working (or not working) well below their potential, will need further general education as well as further technical or specialist training if they are to have a passport to a better job at a higher level of skill. Continuing adult education and training becomes in this decade not a Cinderella service for adult institutes, but a mainstream activity of great prestige and importance.

In the meantime, while these developments are gradually beginning to happen, government has started up another important initiative – Enterprise in Higher Education (EHE). This was launched in 1987 and is run by the Training Agency. By the summer of 1990, the majority of the UK's largest higher education institutions will be taking part in it.

EHE is, in very general terms, a kind of TVEI for higher education. Many of the same ingredients are there – partnerships with employers, work-related curricula, work experience for students and staff, enterprising teaching and learning styles, accreditation of personal effectiveness as well as academic achievement, etc. Here is what Tim Eggar, Minister of State for Employment, says about EHE in the 1989 edition of *Key Features in EHE*:

> The graduates of the 1990s will be expected to have that 'extra ingredient' which allows them to meet the strenuous demands of a modern economy. EHE is beginning to address those expectations. Through mutual consultation and cooperation between higher education and the business world, tomorrow's graduates are gaining the enterprising skills they and the market place need for further success.

In the same document, the Enterprise Curriculum is described thus:

> There are perhaps as many definitions of 'enterprise' as there are people defining the word! However, there is a great deal of common ground, and most people would agree that the enterprising person is resourceful, adaptable, creative, innovative and dynamic. He or she may also be entrepreneurial. However, the qualities of enterprise are as useful in the employee as in the employer, and equally important in the public, private and voluntary sectors.
>
> Transition and change are fundamental to Higher Education. Most students in HE are making the transition from school to adult life, or changing from one career to another. The world for which students are preparing is also changing . . . faster now than ever before. Technological changes mean that one set of skills will no longer last throughout a working life. Changes in employment patterns mean people will change jobs more often, perhaps spending some time in self-employment. Political changes and developments in world markets are giving more jobs an international dimension, making demands on workers' flexibility and ability to communicate and adapt.
>
> Educational institutions are responding to change by changing themselves. Traditional teaching methods are giving way to more participative and activity-based styles of learning, where enterprising qualities are encouraged and rewarded. A growing number of programmes and activities are introducing secondary pupils to the 'enterprise curriculum'. In the

Technical & Vocational Education, Mini Enterprise Projects, and the RSA's Education for Capability scheme, practical experience and real-life problem-solving are taking their place alongside 'chalk and talk'. YTS and school work experience programmes have opened up new partnerships between employers and educationalists. The aim of the Enterprise in Higher Education initiative is to foster and develop this enterprise curriculum in higher education.

This is a tall order but one which higher education has tackled enthusiastically and – dare I say it – with great enterprise. As it enters its third year, the EHE initiative is raising important questions about the needs of students and their prospective employers, and about the kind of education higher education students will need to face the challenges of the 1990s. It promises to be an exciting time for higher education.

Reference

Enterprise in Higher Education: Key features of the EHE proposals 1988–9. Sheffield: The Training Agency, 1989.

10

Apocalypse Now? Where Will Higher Education Go in the Twenty-first Century?

Peter Slee

Everyone does it at the dawn of a new decade, and I am no exception. I offer three predictions: the first for 100 years ahead; the second for 20 years ahead; and the third too close for comfort. Needless to say, the boldness of the projections is in inverse proportion to the likelihood of my telephone ringing to tell me I was wrong.

First, the late twenty-first century. The historian who in 2090 writes the definitive study of the 1980s will allocate little positive significance to higher education policy. He will identify two policy strands: instrumentalism and retrenchment. But he will note that both were ill-conceived, and that, as a result, neither caused change of lasting or deep significance to the higher education system. Certainly, he will note there *were* changes at the interface between higher education and its three client groups: students, employers and government. Retrenchment will have caused a clear shift in the nature of the job of the registrar, from administration of a stable system, to self-conscious proactive management of declining resources (this trend is well illustrated by Bosworth, 1986; Hayward, 1986; Temple and Whitchurch, 1989). And even as departments became budget centres, instrumentalism raised to common currency among academics the language of cost-benefit and measurement. Transferable personal skills, competencies and added-value became integrated in most departmental heads' returns, reports and promotions.

Increased significance was attached to communication with employers and alumni. But in the 1980s, this mostly involved turning up the volume on existing channels and making statements of principle rather than engaging in dialogue. So, changes yes, but historical analysis and hindsight will show that these were changes of style, not substance. In the 1980s, there was no radical change in the culture of higher education; and no major shift in perceived function. Indeed, the book will show that the reverse was true. Confused policy initiatives engendered powerful reaffirmation of cultural mores, and the strengthening of belief in traditional functions.

The value system bequeathed by Robbins – education, research, instruction and culture (ERIC) – prevailed over notions of enterprise, retrenchment, national goals and instrumentalism (ERNI). ERIC offered all teachers in higher education a positive belief in a multifunctional role – not just for the system or for their institution, but for themselves. The upshot was the continued dominance of the traditional central organizing principle of higher education, the discipline. The discipline, the historian will suggest, was to higher education what that curious artefact the Swiss army knife had been to generations of explorers. It performed adequately across a range of functions. Specialist tools would have done each individual job to a more professional standard. But they cost more, were heavier to carry around, and could always be hired to finish the job if really needed. When ERIC was the goal for all students in publicly funded higher education, only the discipline would do, and only disciplinary specialists had the breadth and depth of knowledge to do the jobs it entailed (for a classic statement of this view, see the words of Charles Oman in Slee, 1986).

Second, prediction. In 20 years' time, the British system of higher education will not exist in its present shape and form. The future will be a country with whose language we are now unfamiliar. But the revolutionary shift will not result from the proactive policy of radical governments or the ideas of crusading social theorists, but from a defensive response to the impact of three trends now on an irreversible collision course.

The first trend involves what is currently the primary consumer of higher education, the 18-year-old. Having become something of a scarce commodity between 1983 and 1996, in 1977 the 18-year-old will be on the increase until reaching a stabilizing peak between the years 2005 and 2010 (Smithers and Robinson, 1989, pp. 14–19). At first sight, then, a significant rise in the cohort of potential students, which taken in conjunction with the outcome of current demographic trends currently helping to raise participation rates in higher education, looks promising for universities, colleges and polytechnics.

The second trend also raises optimism. For in the year 2005 the predictions of Professor Handy will have come to pass. There will be 'no place for unskilled workers in any organisation. Their unskilled contribution simply [does] not add value to pay their wages.' Britain's future will, self-evidently, rest heavily on the creation of a highly skilled, highly paid, highly productive workforce making things 'smarter and better' than the rest (Handy, 1989). And that, in turn, means educating and training smarter and better than the rest. The upshot is that the new cohort of 18-year-olds will all need positively to be educated and trained to higher standards in order simply that they are fit to pay their way. And there is more, for some 80% of the workforce in the year 2005 will have been in gainful employment since the 1980s (CBI, 1988). They, too, will need smartening and bettering to remain in productive employment. The labour market role for higher education in the reduction of skill shortages will never have been clearer. But what is happening in higher education in this hour of need? It is suffering the biggest skill shortage of all. For while two trends are contriving to raise demand for teaching, the third has reduced the supply of teachers by over 70%. In 1990, the average age of the British academic is 44. Over 70% are aged between 45 and 55 (*Times Higher Educational Supplement*, 19 January 1990). There will be no steady trickle of retirements, but a dam-burst sweeping the accumulated expertise of four decades with it, and taking the government of the day back to the drawing board.

So, higher education in the year 2010 will be different. But how, and in what way? The answer is completely, and in three ways.

First, a new pattern of institutional provision will emerge. It will have two key features.

1. Half of the institutions we know in the 1990s will lose their identity through closure or merger. There will be little choice. As the survivors of the post-war baby boom begin to collect their pensions, the government will be unable to maintain levels of expenditure on higher education. And, even were resources to be found for expansion, the cohort from which dons would be drawn is that which will form the trough of the demographic downturn of the 1970s. Higher education will become leaner by accident, rather than by design.

2. Higher education provision will be sharply defined into four sectors. First, a dozen 'Ivy Leaguers', offering old-fashioned, traditional 3- to 4-year residential programmes leading to honours degrees in a broad range of disciplines. They will cater for the traditional student market. Second, a dozen giant civics offering a range of services tailored flexibly to the needs of a range of regionally based clientele. Third, a national network of distance- and open-learning centres covering professional updating, training and development. And, finally, a handful of specialist research institutions.

Second, finance. The leaner higher educational system will be geared to the market. All young people aged 16–21 years, and most employees, will carry an entitlement towards assisted personal development. Institutions will pull in the 60% of their income needed to pay salaries entirely from the vouchers and fees recouped from their clients.

Third, qualification and assessment structure. Qualifications will be streamlined within an overarching system of post-compulsory education and development. Degrees will be modularized. Credit accumulation and transfer, and accreditation of work-based learning, will become the central tiers of the system. The 18- to 21-year-olds will form a minority among those profiting from higher education. Only the Ivy Leaguers will stand apart from the trend.

In the 1990s, the name of the winning game will be marketing. Only high-quality institutions will remain intact in the first decade of the next century. But as Sir Christopher Ball (1985) has put it, 'What the hell is quality?' None other than fitness for purpose. There will be three key elements in a successful marketing strategy:

- Reading the market and targeting a niche in it.
- Giving one's product brand identity and positioning it within the niche market.
- Knowing the value of one's product. Pricing will not be a function of manufacturing costs but a function of value to the customer.

Potential Ivy Leaguers will begin to tighten their grip on the traditional

18-year-old, 3-year residential market. They will market a package: high social status, attractive surroundings, collegiality, and a reputation for high-quality research across a range of disciplines.

Selectivity will be maintained partially through high fees well above the average value of vouchers or entitlements, artificially high entrance requirements formulated in terms of traditional school-leaving certificates, and high levels of support from the potential employers of their graduates. Potential civics will begin to consolidate their range of functions: continuing education, professional updating, credit accumulation and transfer, distance-learning and access courses. Full-time degrees and research will begin to be concentrated in selected departments receiving additional top-up funding from new sources. Networking will begin among institutions within distinct geographical locations in an attempt to co-ordinate campaigns to attract a new clientele to higher education.

In the 1990s, more *will* mean different (Ball and Eggins, 1989). But not for everyone and not in every way. Knowing how different you *want* to be, and recognizing how different you *have* to be, will mark the distinction between leader and led. The leaders will already have defined their product and have begun marketing their brand image to employers, niche communities, and government.

In the 1990s we may see the collapse of the binary system, but the status gap between institutions will grow. Fitness for purpose suggests parity of esteem. But in the 1990s, some institutions will be more equal than others. And they will be those whose culture and functions are more ERIC than ERNI.

References

Ball, C. (1985). What the hell's quality? In Urwin, D. (ed.), *Fitness for Purpose*, pp. 96–102. Nelson: SRHE/NFER.

Ball, C. and Eggins, H. (eds) (1989). *Higher Education into the 1990s: New Dimensions*. Milton Keynes: SRHE/Open University Press.

Bosworth, S. (ed.) (1986). *Beyond the Limelight: Essays on the Occasion of the Silver Jubilee of the Conference of University Administrators*. CUA.

Confederation of British Industry (1988). *Skills for Success: The 1988 CBI Training Presentation*. London: CBI.

Handy, C. (1989). Missing ingredient. *Times Higher Educational Supplement*, 10 March, p. 26.

Hayward, J. (1986). Responses to contraction: The University of Hull, 1979–1984. *Minerva*, **XXIV**(1), 74–98.

Slee, P. (1986). *Learning and a Liberal Education: The Study of Modern History in the Universities of Oxford, Cambridge and Manchester 1800–1914*. Manchester: Manchester University Press.

Smithers, A. and Robinson, P. (1989). *Increasing Participation in Higher Education*. BP International.

Temple, P. and Whitchurch, C. (eds) (1989). *Strategic Choice: Corporate Strategies for Change in Higher Education*, pp. 229–37. CUA/APA.

Times Higher Educational Supplement (1990). 19 January, p. 1.

The Society for Research into Higher Education

The Society exists both to encourage and co-ordinate research and development into all aspects of higher education, including academic, organizational and policy issues; and also to provide a forum for debate – verbal and printed.

The Society's income derives from subscriptions, book sales, conference fees, and grants. It receives no subsidies and is wholly independent. Its corporate members are institutions of higher education, research institutions and professional, industrial, and governmental bodies. Its individual members include teachers and researchers, administrators and students. Members are found in all parts of the world and the Society regards its international work as among its most important activities.

The Society is opposed to discrimination in higher education on grounds of belief, race etc.

The Society discusses and comments on policy, organizes conferences, and encourages research. Under the imprint SRHE & OPEN UNIVERSITY PRESS, it is a specialist publisher of research, having some 40 titles in print. It also publishes *Studies in Higher Education* (three times a year) which is mainly concerned with academic issues; *Higher Education Quarterly* (formerly *Universities Quarterly*) mainly concerned with policy issues, *Abstracts* (three times a year); an *International Newsletter* (twice a year) and *SRHE News* (four times a year).

The Society's committees, study groups and branches are run by members (with help from a small secretariat at Guildford). The groups at present include a Teacher Education Study Group, a Staff Development Group, and a Continuing Education Group and a Women in Higher Education Group. The groups may have their own organization, subscriptions, or publications (e.g. the *Staff Development Newsletter*). A further *Questions of Quality* Group has organized a series of Anglo-American seminars in the USA and the UK.

The Society's annual conferences are held jointly; 'Access and Institutional Change' (1989, with the Polytechnic of North London). In 1990, the topic will be 'Industry and Higher Education' (with the University of Surrey). In 1991, the topic will be 'Research and Higher Education', with the University of Leicester; in 1992, it will be 'Learning and Teaching' (with Nottingham Polytechnic). Other conferences have considered 'HE After the Election' (1987) and 'After the Reform Act' (July 1988).

The Editorial Board of the Society's imprint seeks authoritative research or study in the field. It offers competitive royalties, a highly recognizable format in both hardback and paperback and the world-wide reputation of the Open University Press.